GRAVE EXODUS

GRAVE EXODUS

Tending to Our Dead in
the Twenty-first Century

XAVIER A. CRONIN

BARRICADE BOOKS INC. / NEW YORK

Published by Barricade Books Inc.
150 Fifth Avenue
New York, NY 10011
Copyright © 1996 by Xavier A. Cronin

Book design and page layout by CompuDesign

Printed in the United States of America.

Library of Congress Cataloging-in-Publication Data

Cronin, Xavier A.
Grave exodus : tending to our dead in the 21st century /
        by Xavier A. Cronin.
ISBN 1-56980-095-2
1. Funeral supplies industry—United States—Forecasting.
2. Undertakers and undertaking—United States—Forecasting.
3. Funeral rites and ceremonies—United States—Forecasting.
4. Twenty-first century—Forecasts.   I. Title.
HD9999.U53U526 1996
393' .0973—dc20   96-8704
                                                          CIP

First Printing

CONTENTS

ACKNOWLEDGMENTS

This book would not have been possible without the help and guidance of my colleague Nick Verrastro. I'm also indebted to the many funeral directors and cemeterians I've interviewed over the past four years.

I could mention many people, but I would be remiss if I didn't personally thank Ed Laux, Sumner Brashears, John Blake, Lisa Carlson, Larry Anspach, Tom Sherrard, Jerri Lyons, and Tom Weber, who spent lots of time answering my questions.

Finally, thanks to my agent, Julie Castiglia, for her guidance and perseverance.

A WORD ON THE TEXT

Some still call them undertakers, but the people who sell and perform funerals are by and large called funeral directors or morticians. They work at funeral homes or mortuaries, although many people call them "funeral parlors." The parlor comes from the days when people laid out their dead in the parlor of their home. Mortuary and mortician are used more often in the West.

This book uses funeral director and mortician interchangeably. When undertaker is used, it is in sections on the history of America's funeral industry.

Funeral directors refer to each body they get as a "call" or a "case," as in, "John Doe Funeral Home did 200 calls (cases) last year."

"Cremains" is used to refer to cremated remains, what's left after a body is incinerated for a few hours at about 1,800 degrees and churned to a grainy powder the consistency of sand, usually in an electric contraption that looks like a big metal blender. "Cremains" is used widely in the death industry and by many newspapers.

Three words I have coined for this book:

Casketeer—identifying casket manufacturers, consultants, and sales people.

Memorialite—referring to members of the country's 140 memorial and funeral society death cooperatives.

Cryptonite—used in Chapter six to identify those entombed in a mausoleum crypt (not be confused with the only substance that can kill Superman).

I use *Cremationist* to refer to a variety of people, including those advocating cremation, those selling cremation services, and people who've chosen to be cremated and have a strong feeling about why they've done so. *Cremationist* and *Crematist* were first used in the late nineteenth century to identify the pioneers of America's cremation movement.

A *cemeterian* is someone who owns or operates a cemetery, but it can also refer to others who work at cemeteries in various capacities.

Pay-before-you-die and *preneed* are used interchangeably. They refer to the funeral and cemetery policies people buy before, of course, they die. The *need* in *preneed* is used as in "your time of need," or "When you die, you'll have a need for what you should buy before you die." The same use of *need* is employed in the death industry euphemism, "at-need," meaning you're buying the funeral, cremation, grave, mausoleum crypt, etc. after someone has died *at* the time of need. Funeral preneed is a huge industry that has emerged in the past twenty years or so.

Prearrangement means you've arranged but not necessarily paid for post-death products and services before the great event occurs. Most people agree it makes sense to buy or arrange these matters before you die, with the exception of funeral directors who would rather negotiate at-need, the way it's still done in many parts of the country, and the way most funeral business was conducted until about twenty years ago.

A "memorial park" is a fancy cemetery with lots of flat and gently rolling open space, usually without all the big tombstones, statues, busts, and other artwork found at many cemeteries.

An *Alternative Container* is a cheap cardboard or fiberboard box dead people are cremated in. It is the designation given by the federal government, which requires funeral homes to make them available to people in case they don't want to spend a lot of money on a casket.

INTRODUCTION

Americans are getting cremated, more than half a million of us each year, of all faiths and backgrounds, in thousands of cremation chambers at 1,100 crematories across the country. That's about one cremation for every five deaths. By the year 2010, the ratio will be about one cremation for every three deaths, and some time in the middle of the twenty-first century, as the last of the 76 million baby boomers die, the cremation rate is expected to peak at 50 or 60 percent.

This exodus from the grave—what you might call the Cremating of America—is the manifestation of changing death mores that question the tradition of spending thousands of dollars on dignifying a corpse with embalming and cosmetics and putting it in a casket, itself often sealed in a vault, and finally lowering it into a hole in the ground for eternity. On another level, it is the raw working of the marketplace: A service is being offered and people are buying.

Indoor cremation in America—as opposed to the outdoor funeral pyre still common in India and other countries—is 120 years old. The first one was conducted in 1876 by an eighty-year-old doctor who decided the best way to bring attention to the folly and waste of flamboyant funerals and the health hazards of putting dead bodies in the ground was to promote his own cremation in a cremation chamber he built himself. By 1970 the cremation rate had grown to just 4 percent of our annual dead, with many cremations occurring on the West Coast. Some states didn't even have crematories, and mainstream Americans generally buried their dead without a second thought. Then a phenomenon called direct cremation took hold in California in the early 1970s and spread rapidly across most of the country.

The cremation rate hovers at about 21 percent nationwide —of 2,286,000 deaths in 1994, 469,000 were cremations— and it is rising everywhere but areas of the Bible Belt, where religion and tradition and plenty of burial space make folks bullish on burial. Cremation is generally higher in cities— Chicago has a 35 percent cremation rate, the state of Illinois is at 15 percent—and lower in rural America. In some areas, the rise has been dramatic, like Idaho, where it has more than doubled, from 13 percent to 32 percent, in the last ten years, and California, which cremates 43 percent of its dead.

The arrival of cremation as a competitor to burial has not been welcome news for the country's approximately 23,000 funeral homes, which depend on bodies for business. Eighty percent of cremations are "direct disposals," or "pick-up-and-burns," as they are called in the industry, in which the body goes straight from place of death to a cremation furnace without embalming, casket, flowers, funeral, urn, or committal service. The funeral director has been removed from the process. In the old days of just a generation ago, a death almost always meant a funeral and a burial. When someone died, the biggest decision the family had to make was often what kind of casket to buy—metal or wood. Today, many survivors left with post-death chores, or the dead themselves, as prescribed in a cremation service bought in advance, are choosing quick and tidy cremations for as little as three of four hundred dollars, which includes the cardboard box or cheap casket the deceased is to be cremated in and the plastic box for the "cremains," an often-used abbreviation for cremated remains. Compare this amount with the $5,100 average cost of a funeral with merchandise, which doesn't include grave plot, headstone, gravedigging, and other charges at the burial ground.

The key to success for the death industry in the emerging era of cremation is, as you would expect, getting people to spend more on it. After years of fighting cremation, the industry pretty much threw in the towel at the end of the 1980s, and now there's a scramble on from all quarters for a piece of the ever-expanding cremation dollar.

The stakes are high: The business of death has become big business in the last half of the twentieth century. It is now an estimated $12 billion a year industry, with $8 billion on the funeral side and $4 billion on the cemetery side, and cremation spread between them. The publicly owned "death care" corporations, as they call themselves, own nearly 20 percent of the country's mortuaries and 600 or so cemeteries. The largest, Service Corp. International (SCI) of Houston, owns about 2,900 funeral homes around the world (including 534 in Great Britain and more than 1,000 in France) and 320 cemeteries with total 1995 revenue of $1.6 billion. With 32 percent of its North American market comprised of cremation, and a 70 percent cremation rate in England, SCI made it clear to shareholders in its 1995 annual report that "The Company believes that the memorialization of cremated remains represents a source of revenue growth. Since the number of cremations is increasing, the Company is emphasizing the marketing of memorialization alternatives."

Most everybody in the death industry has jumped on the cremation bandwagon in recent years. Cremation used to be a four-letter word to funeral directors. Today cremation consultants are teaching cremation merchandising to cremation-minded morticians with more and more "cremation families" as clients. Membership in the country's national cremation trade association has doubled in the past decade. Strictly cremation "cremation society" businesses have sprung up across the country—type in "cremation" for a World Wide Web Webcrawler search and find dozens of their home pages. Burial vault companies, comprising a $1.2 billion chunk of the death business, are pushing urn vaults, little metal boxes offering a second layer of protection for the cremains. Casket companies are marketing quick-burning cremation or crematable caskets and expanding their urn lines.

New in the fall of 1995, from perhaps the country's top cremation casket maker, Elder-Davis Inc., was the First Step elite cremation cardboard box. Batesville Casket, the $500 million manufacturer, set up a cremation division in 1994 specializing in cremation caskets and urns. Batesville sells about a million caskets a year and taps cremation's environmental appeal by planting trees in national forests in memory of those incinerated in their cremation caskets.

The enemy to everyone is direct disposal, although some mortuaries charge more than $1,500 for it, in essence saying they're not going to work for a few hundred bucks just because someone wants a pick-up-and-burn.

WHY WE'RE GETTING CREMATED

Cremation is cheaper and our cemeteries are running out of land. These are the most common reasons given by the media and consumer groups for our exodus from the grave. It's also the perception of many laypeople I've talked to in the last two and a half years. They are major reasons, but there are many others (some we'll never know).

Cremation certainly forces consideration of a postconsciousness existence. British author Bertram Puckle put it succinctly in 1926: "We cannot give even a few moments of serious thought to cremating as opposed to earth burial without being forced to define our *real* [his italics] beliefs concerning an existence after death. Even orthodox minds may be surprised to discover how little assurance they have when faced with the possibilities of a conscious sacrifice of their bodies to the flames." For those choosing cremation and banking on an afterlife, or some kind of postconsciousness existence, cremation presupposes a belief that it doesn't matter what's done to a dead body; that the chance of entering Heaven or some great astral plane isn't diminished if the body is prematurely reduced to calcium, rather than allowing decomposition to work its course. This was the attitude of our first "Cremationists," covered in Chapter three, and it may be the underlying attitude of many of us today.

Cremation is cheaper than a funeral and burial, unless you choose a high-end affair, say, a gold-plated urn and premium niche stored in a prestigious location, like the dome-topped Neptune Society Columbarium in San Francisco. Chartering a plane for aerial scattering can also boost the cost of a fiery farewell. Many of today's cremationists are middle-class people thinking purely in terms of saving money, unlike the early days of cremation when many choosing it were intellectuals and eccentrics making personal statements about death, the after-life, and the vanity of funeral and burial. Today, the creed of the Cremation Everyman advises: *Why not leave the money you'd spend on a casket and funeral and grave and all the trim-mings to survivors or a worthy cause, or use the money while you still have time?*

When I asked sixty-five-year-old Jane Tuck, secretary of the San Antonio Memorial Society, why most of her members choose cremation, she said: "We just buried my mother and mother-in-law. Both [funerals] cost six thousand dollars a piece. It seemed like a foolish waste of money. Here in San Antonio, a cremation is under five hundred dollars. People have expensive funerals to keep up with the Joneses." Tuck's group is one of America's 140 memorial or funeral societies, covered in Chapter nine, not to be confused with the for-profit "cremation societies." They are essentially death cooperatives bargaining with mortu-aries for cheap rates. The largest is People's Memorial Society in Seattle, formed in 1939 by a left-wing minister preaching the "Socialistic Gospel." People's has 110,000 members (each paying a $10 membership fee) and sends 200 bodies a month to Seattle's Bleitz Funeral Home/Crematory, which cremates 90 percent of them for $471 each ($11 extra for a death cer-tificate). The handful choosing burial pay $728 for funeral (including embalming) and a cheap, cloth-covered wooden casket, or they spend a few hundred dollars more for a "casket upgrade." Compare with the $20,000 high-end funeral package at D. O. McComb & Sons Funeral Homes in Fort Wayne, Indiana, which includes a gold-plated bronze casket, selling alone for $17,324. Or the $24,000 bronze casket at Chicago's Theis-Gorski Funeral Home, or perhaps the country's most expensive casket, a bronze monster going for $85,000 at the prestigious Frank E. Campbell Funeral Home on the Upper East Side of Manhattan (1994 prices).

The space issue is really an environmental issue: People think it's absurd and irresponsible to stuff another space-hogging corpse into the bowels of a hopelessly overpopulated planet. "We're very concerned with our land here, and we think there are better things to do than put dead bodies in it," says Patricia Clark, an officer of the Central Coast Memorial Society in San Luis Obispo, California. As for a scarcity of cemetery space, many urban burial grounds are cramped, but with plenty of space in suburbia and rural areas, many cemeteries are turning to inside interment. Mausoleums with room for hundreds and thousands of bodies are going up around the country. The largest is Mission Mausoleum at Inglewood Park Cemetery in Los Angeles: 30,000 crypts in aboveground and underground levels. This burial-bullish cemetery has nearly 100,000 individual crypts in mausoleums and catacombs built under parking lots.

Another reason for our grave exodus: the same ongoing social change we've heard so much about in recent years—our "mobile" society and the "breakup of the nuclear family." Families are spread out, and as harsh as it may sound, when someone dies it's not always convenient or desirable to fly everyone or the body itself to a central location for a funeral. The sad truth may be that nobody really cared much for a distant aunt or uncle who just passed away. Another factor is longevity: People are living longer than ever these days, and some simply outlive all their friends and family. Why spend thousands on casket and funeral and burial if no one's going to be there but a funeral director, clergy, and the gravedigger? "There's no point in putting bodies in the ground," says Bob Jones, president of People's Memorial Society. "People are so mobile, families move around, what use is there for a family plot?"

As for the folks who tend to our dead, about 80,000 or so morticians and trade embalmers, as well as tens of thousands of memorial counselors and others working at cemeteries, they are being told by their association leaders, consultants, and corporate bosses that they'd best jump on the cremation bandwagon lest they be left behind in the ash heap of another era.

1

AMERICA'S ANNUAL DEATH MERCHANDISING EXTRAVAGANZA

The bodies of the newly dead are not debris nor remnant, nor are they entirely icon or essence. They are, rather, changelings, incubates, hatchlings of a new reality that bear our names and dates, our images and likenesses as surely in the eyes and ears of our children and grandchildren as did word of our birth in the ears of our parents and their parents. It is wise to treat such new things tenderly, carefully, with honor.

—Thomas Lynch, essayist/funeral director

*B*etween shiny new hearses and embalming displays are the caskets—scores of caskets laid out for browsing funeral directors in this huge exhibition hall stretching the length of a football field.

They are made of oak, pine, mahogany; steel, bronze, copper; plastic, teakwood, fiberglass. There are cheap cloth-covered caskets made of fiberboard, miniature units for children, and rental caskets loaded with a cardboard box insert in which the body is delivered to the crematory.

Interiors are velvet, satin, or chiffon, in pinks, blues, and whites. One is lined with an Indian village drawn on buckskin denim. A few rotate on elevated platforms. Some rest in giant rust-colored vaults, added protection for the body from air, water, and ground critters, and which ensure the casket remains in its rightful place, two, four, six, or even nine feet under, should it splinter into pieces. There's been more than a few lawsuits filed after some unlucky mortal wandering through a cemetery tumbled into a compromised grave.

Retail prices for the caskets range from a few hundred dollars for the fiberboards, to $700 for a quick-burning poplar, destined for the flames of the cremation chamber, to $20,000 for a gold-plated bronze masterpiece. Flanking the caskets on all sides are salesmen in suits—virtually all of them white, thirty to seventy years old. They stand in small groups chatting and smiling with funeral directors, some 5,000 gathered here at the National Funeral Directors Association's (NFDA) 1993 annual fall convention and merchandising expo, held this year in Chicago.

Sharing center stage on the blue-carpeted floor are hearses and minivans. Doors are open, side and back, demonstrating ease-of-loading. From somewhere comes singing, a solo baritone soaring above the murmur of the crowd. It's Merrill Womach, president of National Music Service Company, one of the country's largest providers of recorded music for mortuaries. Womach, a middle-aged man with white hair and a disfigured face (from a plane crash), wearing a black tuxedo, is performing a melancholy tune. Strapped on her back to an embalming table is a 30ish woman with bleached-blond hair and lots of makeup. Her large dark eyes are open wide, looking up at the rafters. She's playing the corpse to demonstrate something called a "T-strap," a gizmo for positioning bodies. She brings to mind another blond woman I saw at my first death show, in San Antonio in 1992: an attractive, young local model, working for the Nadine Cosmetics Company of Russellton, Pennsylvania, demonstrating makeup for the dead, smearing it on the outstretched hands of browsers. Nadine's brochure explains that its "lip rouge" comes in "five colors, and will not only match existing colors, but can be used to highlight or neutralize certain 'problem' areas."

Nearby a booth displays the Extremities Positioner. Like the T-strap, it's a product for the funeral home "prep room," as it's called in the trade, where the dead are readied for a final appearance. The extremities positioner is a looped rope used for tying the hands of big bodies together so they don't slide off the stomach while survivors take a final look during the funeral "visitation" or, in the parlance of yesteryear and traditionalists, the wake. Standing at the booth is Bernard Yonke, a funeral director from Pewaukie, Wisconsin. "This is a good product, I'll tell ya," says Bernard, a stocky man wearing a checkered blazer standing next to a stuffed clown propped on a chair. A sign next to the clown reads, "It's No Joke—We're Not Clowning Around!" an attention-getter for passers-by who may have been kicking a few tires or chatting with a vault salesman. Bernard's in a festive mood, smiling and shaking our hands vigorously, assuring us morticians would welcome this new product. (The number of obese dead was increasing—at least they'd been for Bernard.)

The extremities positioner brochure reads:

> After encountering remains in excess of 300 pounds, Mr. Yonke knew something with strength was needed to position and maintain the position of extremities during repose. The positioner will eliminate the use of newspaper, cotton, or other fillers to hold the hands in position.

I suggest a demonstration. My colleague, Nick Verrastro, volunteers. Bernard slips the little white rope around his wrists and smiles: "I've never had a complaint yet." Nick—in his seventh year as editor of the trade magazines I work for, *American Funeral Director* and *American Cemetery*—poses deadpan for a few snapshots, arms extended like a prisoner about to be frisked. We exchange pleasantries, Nick is untied, and we set out to explore some of the other 200 exhibits.

"This place gives me the creeps," says Nick, who's seen enough Frigid Fluid, crypt liners and "those death dresses," as he calls the burial gowns hanging from racks throughout the exhibit, to wonder what happened to the good old days when he wrote for a travel magazine. Creeps or no creeps, this is Nick's fifth death show, and he knows it's part of our convention coverage ritual to survey the exhibits.

The Forethought Group preneed insurance booth trumpets, "Total Casket Protection": Buy your casket today, with complete funeral package, and the price will be eternally locked in at today's price no matter how long it takes the policy holder to die. It's an attractive selling point for funeral directors looking to lock in the many dollars coming the industry's way as tens of millions of baby boomers hit their 50s and prepare for the inevitable by buying their final purchase ahead of time. People have been buying their graves in advance for years— sometimes as family plots or mausoleum crypts—but the time to buy a funeral used to almost always come "at-need," to use the industry euphemism, meaning when the person is dead, and survivors are saddled with buying a casket and making all the other arrangements.

In the last twenty years, the insurance and funeral industries have changed this situation, teaming up to create a huge pay-before-you-die sub-insurance industry, with an estimated $20 billion in outstanding preneed contracts throughout the country. Death industry giant Service Corp. International lists $2.3 billion in preneed contracts. "Millions arranging for their own funerals," reads a November 1995 *Baltimore Sun* article. "Increasing numbers of Americans are settling the details long beforehand and prepaying for their funerals."

Meandering by hardwood caskets, Nick and I trace the fine lacquer finish with our fingers before arriving at the Madelyn Company table. Here we find "cremation keepsake pendants" and "decorative vessels." Booth-minder Lisa Saxer Buros shows us the locket around her neck in which she keeps a pinch of— who else?—Madelyn, that is, a bit of Madelyn's cremains. Cremains are what's left after your body has been reduced to a pile of bones and is subsequently ground up in a blenderlike contraption or mashed to bits manually by a crematory worker pounding them with a mini sledge hammer or other such tool. What remains is a gray grainy powder with flakes of white, usually five to seven pounds worth, the texture of sand.

One of Madelyn's competitors—a company called Companion Star—makes glass sculptures with shreds of cremains embedded in the glass. This "wearable urn jewelry," as it's sometimes called, was popularized in the late 1980s in San Francisco's Ghia Gallery, a death-chic boutique. The Madelyn in question is Buros' mom. She had died recently and was the inspiration for the company. Now daughter carries a bit of mother in a pendant around her neck. This may seem strange, but throughout history various members of our species have worn and displayed chunks, shards, and shreds of fellow humans, as tokens of remembrance and affection or as trophies. The head has always been a favorite. America's most familiar postmortem head piece collected for show is probably the White Man's scalp, a prized trophy of Indians. Headhunters went for the whole head, boiling and shrinking them and tying them on to their belts. Victorians settled for hair—snipping locks from loved ones' heads and framing them. Children from Thailand preferred bones, bits of their dead king deposited in gold lockets worn around their necks.

After a brief pause at Madelyn's, we move on to Lotty, an elderly woman with a great set of big white teeth and red-polished nails. She stands by five satin gowns on hangers clipped to curtains above a table lined with what looks like ballet slippers. This is the Ethel Maid burial clothes exhibit. These are gowns and slippers for the dead. Lotty is Ethel Maid's veteran saleswoman. In the old days, she tells us, she trekked door-to-door selling gowns, slippers, and suits to funeral directors. Her road career ended one day when she got into an accident during a storm on the way to a funeral home.

Companies making and selling clothes for the dead have been around for years. In 1919, the J. W. McCamish Company in Winchester, Indiana, was offering "a most elaborate and dainty display of burial shoes, silk net and chiffon throws and slumber robes." The tailor there was Mrs. J. W. McCamish. Like Lisa Saxer Buros, it was the death of her mother that inspired the business. When Mrs. McCamish's mom died, she made her a pair of "soft little handmade burial slippers." From then on she made a habit of providing burial slippers for friends. "Her gifts were met with such sincere appreciation that it became an established custom on her part to send these little remembrances to her friends, and when, after following this practice for some years, she was confined to the hospital for some time, with nothing to occupy her time, she made a large stock."

The Practical Burial Footwear Company, of Columbus, Ohio, was advertising a "men's burial shoe in a modern, conservative design," in a May 1971 trade press ad. Jaeger Funeral Supplies in the Bronx, New York, another death clothier setting up shop each year at the funeral expo, offers underwear for the dead: A set of boxers, T-shirt, and black socks for men; slip, panty, and nylons for women. Jaeger also sells the "Eterna-Crib" styrofoam burial container for stillborns at $25 (1994 price).

From burial wear Nick and I move to embalming chemicals at the booth of the Champion Company, in business for more than a century. I ask if they have any Frigid Fluid, which I had seen advertised in our magazine. Frigid Fluid sparked vulgar jokes around our office and was one of the many strange products I'd been introduced to since taking my job as associate editor of *American Funeral Director* and *American Cemetery* magazines, in October 1992. I figured Frigid Fluid was an embalming chemical—the stuff pumped into your body to "chase" your blood and other fluids out, as one embalming student put it to me, so you can be cleaned, preserved, dressed, cosmetized, and otherwise made presentable for final viewing. It turns out Frigid Fluid is indeed embalming fluid, but it is also the name of a company that makes the same and a competitor of Champion, and the Champion booth-tender later complained to our advertising manager about my misguided curiosity.

At the All-Crematory table stands Cal Wilkerson, a silver-haired man in a dark suit in front of long blue chambers that look like boilers. Behind him is a contraption that looks like a portable washing machine—a state-of-the-art pulverizer, churning post-cremation bones to cremains. Various equipment is used to reduce bones to a consistency for placement in an urn or scattering. One crematory that asked not to be identified for this book has been pulverizing human bones with the same kitchen garbage compactor since 1985. A competitor of All Crematory, Industrial Equipment and Engineering Company, guarantees in a trade press ad that its "ECP-200 Electric Cremains Processor" will "reduce cremains to less than 200 cubic inches, therefore eliminating the need for oversized urns." Industrial's retorts can be loaded at 1,400 degrees Fahrenheit. This lets operators at high-volume crematories reload soon after the bones of the previous cremation are swept out.

All Crematory has installed more than 1,000 of its high-heat furnaces (temperature reaching 2,000 degrees) here and abroad. Cremation equipment manufacturers have their eye on Mexico and China (and other countries traditionally burying the dead) as emerging markets. Many cities throughout the world are running out of burial space and an increasing number of governments and cemeteries are looking to cremation to solve the problem. All Crematory and Industrial Equipment and Engineering are global companies with units as far off as China, which installed its first "All" unit in mid-1995. Mexico, despite a population nearly 100 percent Catholic, a religion bullish on burial, has about fifty All retorts throughout the country. All has big expectations for Mexico. At a gathering of cremationists in 1993 in England—the West's leading cremation nation, with a 70 percent rate—All President Terry Sousa told the faithful in a keynote speech:

> "If there is any place in the world that is probably going to have [a] McCremation chain, like in McDonald's, it will probably be Mexico. There are some smart entrepreneurs in Mexico who see the light. When some of us think of the Latin countries, we still think of the Tequila, the sombrero, etc. There are some sharp people there, and I am positive that in short order they will be able to teach us a few things about cremation practices."

Every year America's leading suppliers of death products and services line up in exhibition halls at conventions like this one. In recent years the industry has been referring to itself as the death care industry. It's believed the name was coined by Frank Stewart Jr., CEO of funeral-cemetery chain Stewart Enterprises, when he was taking his company public in the late 1980s and needed to identify his line of business to Wall Street. The name stuck and it's not uncommon today to see "death-care" in newspaper and magazine articles covering the high cost of dying or cremation's increasing popularity. An economics textbook published in 1996 is titled, *The Death Care Industries in the United States*.

It's not all one big happy family, this "death care" industry, despite the trend of a blending of the funeral, cemetery, and cremation components in the last twenty years. The most striking example of this blend is the rise of the combination cemetery-mortuary-florist-monument shop-chapel. In many areas of the country, one-stop shopping for all your death needs has come to town. But despite such combos and research that shows that the average Joe and Jane believe mortuaries, cemeteries, and crematories are part of the same industry, many in the funeral and cemetery camps believe they are absolutely separate and different animals. When you buy a grave, the proud cemeterian declares, the cemetery promises to take care of it forever, in perpetuity, as they say. Their clients are for life. When you deal with the funeral home, it's over when the body is interred or cremated. Funeral directors point out that much of their business is from families sending them their dead generation after generation.

Cemeteries have been selling their property and services in advance, initially as burial insurance, throughout the century; until recently almost all funerals were arranged and paid for after the person died. The starkest difference is the most obvious: a cemetery is land, a funeral home a building. Many cemeteries have sprawling lawns with mausoleums, statues, monuments, and chapels. They employ grounds professionals while mortuaries need only make sure the lawn is cut (where there is one), the hedges trimmed, and the flowers watered. Most American cities have at least a few well-tended cemeteries and many have sprawling historic burial grounds laid out in the nineteenth century when rural cemeteries replaced graveyards and the country experienced a golden age of mausoleums.

American cemeterians have their own association, the International Cemetery and Funeral Association (ICFA, pronounced ICK-FAH), which had been the American Cemetery Association—formed in 1887 by cemetery superintendents—until it changed its name in 1996 to get more members from the funeral camp.

ICFA puts on its own annual get-together as flamboyant in spirit, if not in numbers, as the funeral show. You'll find a smattering of vaults and urns at the cemetery exhibit and just a few casket companies. Despite the recent phenomenon of casket stores opening in strip malls and a handful of cemeteries selling caskets (in states where it's allowed), the casket remains the sacrosanct merchandise of the funeral director. After all, it was carpenters and cabinet makers hammering out coffins in the seventeenth, eighteenth and nineteenth centuries who often agreed to "under take" the grim business of carting the dead to the graveyard, and who gave themselves the more dignified designations of funeral director and mortician by the end of the nineteenth century. There's historic lineage along with the casket, and today's morticians aren't about to let outsiders snatch away their time-honored merchandise.

So cemeterians have pretty much kept their hands off caskets (except, of course, when they must lower them into the grave or slide them into the cremation chamber).

At the annual cemetery show you'll find specialty companies, like Puckett Supply, which for decades has been making tents (for rainy graveside services) and supplies for the mausoleum, like deodorant powder to freshen up smelly crypts and poison to kill Phorid flies, which detect rotting flesh from miles away and have frustrated not a few mausoleum tenders.

A giant bronze eagle usually rotates center stage at the cemetery exhibit—monument and headstone companies are major suppliers—and browsers can get their shoes shined while sipping drinks, munching finger food, and enjoying a live jazz or Dixieland ensemble. Architects and builders stand by drawings and photos of mausoleums and columbariums. A columbarium can be a free-standing wall in a cemetery or churchyard made of niches—cubby hole compartments holding urns—or an entire building or room, usually part of a crematory complex, dedicated to "inurnment," the cousin of interment.

The cemetery expo is peppered with vaults and urns. Lawn mower companies, such as Toro and John Deere, are here. In recent years computer software has become popular; the entire cemetery can be mapped out on a computer screen, and vital statistics of the dead and those coming (owners of grave plots) are available with a couple of keystrokes. The largest displays come from the monument people, like Matthews International, a publicly traded firm that bought Industrial Equipment & Engineering, the cremation equipment maker, in 1996. In recent years, Matthews has been touting its "Cremorial" ground plots—rectangular bronze boxes for cremains laid out in rows as a metallic columbarium grove. Another space saver from Matthews: the "cremation bench," with four holes under the seat to fasten your urns.

Like the funeral show, the cemetery gathering draws upstarts with quirky new products, like Bernard Yonke's little white rope to lasso the arms of the obese dead. Over the years, the death industry has seen no shortage of products accommodating the dead. A 1909 list of patents shows an "arm rest for corpses," the brainchild of someone called T. Streeter of Tunkharnnock, Pennsylvania, and a "collapsible grave-pillow," patented by James M. and Wilbur I. Doddridge of Milton, Indiana.

At the 1993 cemetery convention in Kansas City, Missouri, the Cremation Casket Company of Omaha displayed miniature wood caskets—finely crafted units like their body-size counterparts. One expects Barbie and Ken in mourning garb next to these six-inch-long boxes. You might want one of these cremation caskets—not to be confused with the full-size cremation caskets covered in the next chapter—after you get the cremains of a loved one and you decide, for whatever reasons, to bury them in a casket. It would be absurd, of course, to put a box full of bones into a body-size casket. Here's the right fit. The little cremation casket has two compartments separated by a sliding panel. Cremains go below and "personal affects"— photos, medals, and jewelry—rest on the cushiony bed above. An element of suspending disbelief is needed at the graveside service as you stand solemnly by this tiny casket about to be lowered into a bite-sized grave. (A check in March 1995 revealed Cremation Casket's phone number disconnected with no referral.)

Another product for the burial of cremains: The "memorial tribute chest," sold at the Cremation Memorial Center of Fred Hunter's Funeral Homes, a 104-year-old funeral/cemetery business in Hollywood, Florida. The chest is for people who own a mausoleum crypt or burial plot and decide, for whatever reasons, to be cremated. Like the little cremation casket, the idea is to have the right size container for your cremains. You may have thought cremation barbaric when you bought a chunk of land for your expired body, but now, mellowed with age and a reexamined view on the body and afterlife, you decide to leave the earth in flames. Rather than worry about having a grossly oversized space, the memorial tribute chest is big enough to hold your cremains and whatever else you'd like to be buried with: golf clubs, bowling balls, baseball gloves, rifles, anything you can fit in a five-by-three box. Once loaded, you're lowered like buried treasure (sorry) into a traditional grave, or slid into a mausoleum crypt, and your eternal space has been properly filled.

THE LAST-MEMORY PICTURE

It's October 1994 at the Opryland Hotel in Nashville and Anna Louise Bongiovi, a funeral director from Raritan, New Jersey, and second cousin to rock star Bon Jovi, is sifting through a rack of lace and satin burial dresses at the "Mrs. Tommy Austin Dresses" booth. "This is the last memory-picture for survivors," says Bongiovi. Her large dark eyes bulge as she speaks in rapid bursts. She's talking about the funeral visitation and open-casket church service. When I ask what kind of customer is drawn to these gowns, she says, as she continues sifting: "Women always love to look beautiful, even when we're dead. We want to go out as a princess, you know? The last impression counts. The last memory-picture counts."

Anna Louise is talking burial gowns here at NFDA's 1994 exhibition with the seventy-nine-year-old proprietor, Susie Austin, a sturdy woman with curly black hair seen on dignified senior citizens exiting beauty parlors. It's a year after the Chicago death show, and Nick has decided to forego the expo on this day.

Susie made her first burial dress in 1949 when a customer wouldn't settle for one from the manufacturer. Scribbling on an order pad next to Susie is her granddaughter, Susan Echols, a pretty, blue-eyed recent college graduate wearing a red blazer clashing starkly with blond bangs.

Anna Louise has made her way to a second rack. "You don't see dresses like this any more. This is all handmade, see?" She lifts a pink dress toward me, all embroidered lace and satin. "This quality of workmanship is almost a lost art. And there's extra yardage. See, here?" Sure enough, the dress carries excess fabric at the hem. "You never know when you'll have obese people, and with this extra material, we can tailor it for them. No one wants to be put in a garment that won't fit. I'll tell ya, this is workmanship."

Anna Louise spends fifteen minutes with the dresses and orders a dozen or so. They'll be shipped from Susie's home in Springfield, Tennessee, to Raritan. Bongiovi says she'll pay about $75 per dress and sell them for $100 to $125. She'll also sell crepe and satin burial slippers. "The tips of the shoes show, so we have to make sure they're pretty, too," Anna Louise explains. Susie smiles and says, "This lady knows her business," and goes on to tell the story of how she got into the burial gown business:

"I started making these in nineteen-forty-nine," she says with a crisp accent. "I was in the funeral business and lived in a funeral home for twenty-one years. And this lady came in the front door, and she wanted a hand-made dress: 'I don't want a factory dress, I want a handmade dress.' So my husband hired me to make the dress. And before I knew it, I was in the dress business. My friends would come and say, 'Susie, send me a dozen dresses.' I've been showin' them since nineteen-forty-nine."

Susie's granddaughter is smiling, her cheeks flushed: "Nanny still does hair"—the hair of women being prepared for viewing—"and she's fixin' to be eighty years old."

Downstairs in the main exhibition hall are two companies displaying caskets and vaults for infants and pre-toddlers (and the occasional pet). McCord Products makes "high-impact polystyrene" (hard plastic) units.

"My kitty's in one of these," says Kay Hanneman, the owner's wife and partner. She's a friendly, plump woman whose face creases in little red wrinkles as she talks and smiles. In a blue denim skirt, cowboy boots, and a silver cowboy boot pin on a plastic convention badge, she looks ready for a line dance. Her Siamese kitty, "Scratch," died at the ripe age of seventeen and was buried in Hanneman's backyard in one of the eighteen-inch units. A funeral director can buy one of these wholesale for $77. For $164, they can move up to McCord's thirty-six-incher.

The other baby/toddler Casketeer, as you might call folks in this line of work, is Cherokee Casket. There's no plastic here, just wood, copper, and steel, elegant models for those who don't want to scrimp. "This is a little pillow that we make, some have blankets like this one," explains Cherokee co-owner Henrietta Mims, standing by a wood casket lined with pink-ribboned crepe, fluffing up the pillow and pulling down the covers. "This is reversible, blue on one end, pink on the other." (Burial vault maker Rocky Mountain Products introduced the "Heartfelt" infant casket-vault combination in early 1995; it comes with a "teddy bear keepsake" to be buried with the infant.) On the low end at Cherokee is the Ponderosa pine box, followed by the Carolina poplar wood unit and the top-of-the-line thirty-two-ounce copper unit, usually retailing for $1,500 to $2,000.

The price of a casket varies widely from mortuary to mortuary. They've always been the biggest money-maker for the mortician, with huge wholesale-retail markups common. This has changed somewhat since passage in 1984 of the federal "Funeral Rule", which requires funeral homes to give funeral shoppers a "general price list," a second one for caskets and a third for "outer burial containers," consisting of burial vaults and "grave liners." The grave liner does just that: lines the casket with concrete or wood slabs, as opposed to the containerization of pricey bronze, copper, and metal vaults.

TIGER

Standing at the Dixie Vault booth at the 1994 funeral show is a short man with a crew cut and the stern demeanor of a fifty-ish football coach. His name tag reads, "Tiger." It's Lowell "Tiger" Lucken, from Murfreesboro, Tennessee. Opening a brochure on Tiger's table reveals a photo of a twelve-gauge steel vault, rusted and besodden with clods of earth. It had just been raised from the grave it was lowered into on May 8, 1957. The caption reads: "Disinterment and removal to another cemetery for reinterment was handled by Ott & Lee Funeral Home of Forest, Mississippi, on June 24, 1986. After more than 29 years, vault, as well as handles, was in excellent condition." Another photo shows a vault disinterred after 52 years; it's also looking good.

Before we return to Tiger, a few words on the history of burial vaults. They evolved from "mortsafes," iron grills placed over British coffins to protect the dead (and the sentiments of survivors) from body snatchers. Early vaults in America were advertised to do the same, as we had our fair share of professional grave robbers into the twentieth century. An ad in the July 1909 *Western Undertaker* for Clark Grave Vault, one of the biggest and oldest vault companies, reads: "It is more burglar proof than any vault," and concludes with the assurance that, "It is not a cistern nor water tank, but a grave vault." Vault companies were proud of the way their units held up after disinterments. "After eighteen years in the ground this Galion and its contents were as perfectly preserved as on the day of burial," reads ad copy for "Galion Cryptorium" vault from a 1929 *American Funeral Director*. In recent years, with cremation's rapid increase, Clark has been pushing urn vaults. Under shiny little metal boxes, the caption of a 1995 Clark trade press ad reads: "Changing Times Call for Metal Urn Vaults from Clark. Like our Burial Vaults, Clark Urn Vaults are made of the highest quality metals. Engineered and guaranteed to keep moisture away. For families concerned about protecting the cremains of a loved one, Clark Urn Vaults are the ultimate in caring for cremains."

Burial and urn vaults now make up a huge subcasket industry. American cemeteries and mortuaries bought about 1.7 million, or $1 billion worth of concrete vaults and their low-end cousin, "grave liners," in 1994. Elite metal vaults pull in more than $100 million a year for manufacturers. The vault makers have their own associations, with one of the oldest and largest being the National Concrete Burial Vault Association.

The vault's basic purpose today can be understood with a simple formula: Casket protects body; Vault protects casket and grave. From the death professional's point of view, burial containers have always been about, odd as it seems, protection. The vault or grave liner is said to be needed to hold the casket in place and maintain the integrity of the spit of land with a big hole in the ground that is the grave plot. With backhoes, bulldozers, dump trucks, lawn mowers, and other heavy equipment rumbling around, and rain and snow soaking the grounds, graves take a beating and will settle unless one of these big holding blocks provides an impenetrable foundation.

Today's vault companies jockey for an edge in their trade

press ads: A Vantage Burial Vault is seen hovering above the earth in space as "the Ultimate Time Capsule . . . Engineered for Eternity," primarily due to "polypropylene, a space age material, allowing us to offer the longest warranties in the industry." A Trigard Vaults & Liners advertisement shows a young boy whispering in the ear of a friend. The caption reads: "Some secrets are meant to be shared . . ." Trigard's secret is that they "listen to their customers," which lets them "make continual improvements and innovations," one being the Trigard's "structured arch." Doric Vaults explains in its ad copy:

> *"Burial vaults have to endure a huge amount of stress under the weight of the earth. Add a backhoe, a dump truck and a tamping machine passing over the grave, and that pressure increases dramatically. As your families deal with their grief, they shouldn't have to endure the added stress of choosing which burial vault is the strongest. That's why Doric vaults are built with strong protection for casketed remains."*

Even when a body has been sealed in a metal casket, many cemeteries still require vaults. "Even if you put a fourteen-gauge copper casket in the grave, most of those have round edges, and there's nobody can pack the earth around it the way it was before it was disturbed," says Lewis Tingley, a cemeterian from Louisville, Kentucky, in the business since 1946. "When the weather comes in, you're going to have holes in there and people, specifically women in high heels, are gonna fall in those holes." The first time Lewis remembers someone falling in a grave was 1937, when he was a youngster spending time at his father's cemetery, where he worked from the late 1940s until he retired in 1984. "We put in the permanent container rule in 1937," he recalls, meaning the requirement that all graves have vaults. "And the reason we put it in is we had someone walking through the cemetery step on one of the oldest graves, and they fell and broke their leg and their pelvis. They sued us for $5,000—back then, that was a lot of money—and they won." More recently, Mary Hamlin, a funeral director in Danville, Kentucky, survived a close call at a mushy grave: "I stepped on that fake green grass around the grave and there was nothing underneath it, and I started going down," she told me. "The minister grabbed my arm and helped me up. I was laughing, and the family was laughing. They said, 'Mary, that's daddy's grave.'"

The burial vault is also meant to be a second layer of protection for the corpse. You never know when there'll be a call for a disinterment—the digging up of human remains—whether it be a skeleton, a pile of bones, a partially decomposed body, or a heavily embalmed body dried to a tautly leathered mummy. Disinterments, or exhumations, usually happen when survivors move their dead to another cemetery, or a construction crew has to make way for a road or building. Check the legal section of your newspaper and eventually you'll likely come across an announcement for the moving of an old, abandoned graveyard asking survivors of the dead to contact the party within so many days or the remains and grave markers will be moved to such-and-such a place, and there's a court order authorizing this.

Sometimes forensic experts need to examine buried remains in cases of foul play. Sometimes there's reason to cast doubt on the identity of the grave's occupant, and a party asks a court to let them find out for sure, as in the recently celebrated cases of John Wilkes Booth and U.S. President Zachary Taylor, whose graves were exhumed. Sometimes nature provides disinterments with a flood or earthquake and bodies are washed away or sandwiched and squashed above ground. Human remains secured in caskets which were themselves secured in vaults stand a good chance of not sliding out, relieving rescuers of the grim task of retrieving them.

I was reluctant to approach Tiger. Experience has taught me that funeral show exhibitors can be a sensitive lot. And

Tiger seemed like a no-nonsense guy who might not appreciate questions from a journalist. In 1993 I asked someone at the All-Crematory booth (Cal wasn't there at the time) what color cremains were and he complained to our advertising manager, the same guy who scolded me for my Frigid Fluid faux pas. The All booth-tender probably thought I was being mischievous (I wasn't).

Another testy encounter came with Lotty, the burial gown saleswoman I met in 1993. I asked her if women were really buried in her gowns. It seemed absurd that these elegant garments would be on a corpse in the damp earth (although they'd be great archaeological finds). I didn't think of the ancient rite of decking out the dead, from Pharaohs to Victorians, and never really thought about the clothes dead people had on at funerals and burials. I've been to just two funerals my entire life, and one was a bodiless memorial service. I figured Lottie's dresses might end up in someone's old clothes chest. I didn't think of logistical problems, like who would remove the dress after the viewing, and what if someone wanted an open casket at the graveside farewell, and the thought that you might get the spooks from having a corpse's garment in the house.

Anyhow, it was a naive, innocent question, but Lotty was not amused. She said she was "dumbfounded" I'd even asked the question. A little scene developed as I tried to explain my idea about the old clothes chest, and the owner came over and told me I should have learned more about the industry before I was hired.

By the time I got to Tiger at the 1994 show, I hadn't asked any contentious questions. I introduced myself by referencing an article I wrote about a Missouri cemetery that washed away during the Midwest floods of 1993, and asked Tiger whether vaults keep bugs and worms out of the casket. He said bugs and worms don't live deep in the ground, so it's a moot point.

I mentioned to Tiger, "A few vaults held their ground and didn't wash away." He wasn't impressed and said something like, "Looks like you didn't know what you were writing about," and went on to explain that vaults doing what vaults are supposed to do would have washed downstream. The ones that held their ground were waterlogged—exactly what's not supposed to happen to vaults.

But I'd broken the ice and in a few minutes Tiger was smiling and we had a short, polite conversation. Toward the end of it, I again mentioned the idea of protection for the body. I'm unable to understand how so much time and effort over the years have been put into this selling point. Surely death is not easy, nor the thought of the decomposition of a loved one's body. But protection for a corpse? Even if you adhere to the Judeo-Christian-Muslim traditions of burial, it is acknowledged that in the end, needless to say, there is always dust. What are we protecting here?

Tiger cut to the bottom line: "You look around here at these products." He motioned to them. "There's nothing here gonna help the dead."

There's more to NFDA conventions than browsing for caskets. Funeral directors have been organized into associations since the 1860s, when they still called themselves undertakers and embalmers. By the turn of the century there was NFDA and many state associations. Blacks had formed their own group, the National Colored Funeral Directors Association (their 1909 convention was scheduled for Louisville). Big issues in the old days were embalming, contagious diseases, getting licensed by state health departments, decking out caskets for fancy wakes, and strengthening the associations.

Today's NFDA convention mixes the extravagant merchandising displays with workshops, seminars, and association business. Pricey media celebrities keynote general sessions to inspire the troops. Ed Bradley of *60 Minutes* got $27,500 in Nashville; political operatives James Carville and Mary Matalin, his wife, got $25,000 in Orlando in 1995; President Bush's Chief of Staff John Sununu got $15,000 in 1992 in San Antonio. Merlin Olson, Robert Novak, Warren Rudman (filling in for pundit Mark Shields, who was only charging $9,000), Fran Tarkenton . . . the list goes on.

NFDA's House of Delegates is the legislative body, with representatives from fifty states. A few years ago it voted to appeal a provision of a federal law that forbids morticians from charging a fee to customers who don't buy caskets from them. NFDA argued that funeral directors count on casket revenue for operating expenses. Doing a funeral without selling a casket throws everything out of whack because most funeral directors have traditionally covered their overhead costs with a great casket markup. So if someone bought their casket elsewhere they tried to make up for it with a "casket handling fee." The heart of the issue goes to the funeral industry's staunch belief that the casket is theirs, and only theirs, to sell. (The appeal was unsuccessful.)

WILBERT'S PARTY

Every year at the NFDA and ICFA conventions, the publicly traded Loewen Group throws elegant receptions with gourmet finger food, open bar, and tuxedoed-and-sequined top-forty bands. Gathered for this bash are a few thousand schmoozing morticians, suppliers, preneed sellers, and a smattering of spouses and trade press. Loewen is the world's second largest death corporation, with a mid-1996 tally of 850 mortuaries and 170 cemeteries where 12,000 people work. What better place to find new funeral homes and cemeteries to acquire than at the national conventions?

Loewen had a brush with death itself in November 1995 after a Mississippi jury awarded a precedent-setting $500 million in compensation and damages to a plaintiff in a breach-of-contract suit against Loewen. A decade of rapid acquisition came to an abrupt halt, Loewen's stock plummeted and the national media documented Loewen's fall. There was talk of Chapter 11 until a $175 million out-of-court settlement was reached and Loewen seemed to have landed on its feet, and was talking about acquiring at least $500 million worth of properties in 1996. Loewen and three other giant death corporations perform somewhere around 20 percent of our funerals. Death has indeed become big business, and the publicly traded mortuary-cemetery companies have become darlings of Wall Street. Institutional investors are looking favorably at the attractive growth factor in this eternal industry that will see demand skyrocket in the twenty-first century as 76 million baby boomers die.

Loewen's convention party is rivaled each year by Wilbert Burial Vault, king of the vault makers. In Nashville, Wilbert's hoedown on a starry night at a place called Smiley Hollow Barn packed them in as the mandolin-led Kentucky Bluegrass Band picked and grinned and funeral directors and guests devoured ribs and corn on the cob and chugged Red Dog beer under a tent near a barn swarming with twirling line dancers. Wilbert's in the business of encasing bodies, but it seems just as at home with cremains. A 1995 trade press ad for its new line of urns shows the back of a man's head with a dark expanse of sky punctuated with a giant sparkling star laid out in front of him. The headline reads: "People are changing the way they want to be remembered—Make sure they don't change who they call." The copy reads:

"We were the first to offer a premium infant vault/casket combination. The first to provide a comprehensive line of concrete urn vaults in a range of quality price points. And, the first to offer service-of-interment for cremated remains . . . With the demands for cremation on the rise, the next ten years will again be marked with change. And again, Wilbert will lead the charge."

When the convention parties are over, there are dozens of workshops and seminars to choose from. They range from new embalming techniques, to how to collect bills in welfare cases, to how to prepare the funeral home for an inspection of the dreaded government regulator, the Occupational Safety and Health Administration. A 1994 workshop on the delicate job of "multitrauma cases" packed in more than 100 for a slide presentation of unfortunate souls killed from gunshot wounds, baseball bats to the head, ice picks to the back, severed body parts in car crashes, and other horrific wounds. Claude Mitchell, a "restorative art" specialist from Cincinnati, a workshop presenter, told me about his most challenging case: a young man who'd been shot in the face point blank with a shotgun by the husband of the woman he got caught sleeping with. The dead man's wife told Claude she and her children needed to see her husband before he was buried. So Claude, a large black man with a warm, wide smile seen on placid, older blues musicians, says he got to work and transformed the man's face from a mangled mesh of flesh and bone to a presentable representation of what had once been.

NFDA trains morticians on protocol for the aftermath of plane crashes, earthquakes, and other disasters when they are called on to identify and embalm victims. An extraordinary effort came when cemeteries in Hardin, Missouri—the one I mentioned to Tiger—and Albany, Georgia, were washed away in the summers of 1993 and 1994, respectively. Hundreds of funeral directors and cemeterians—some flying in from nearby states—as well as coroners, emergency workers, police, the National Guard, and various volunteers, gathered truckloads of bones, skeletons, decaying bodies, caskets, vaults, headstones, and assorted debris from the rivers and soggy fields this macabre cargo was dumped into. They spent months with survivors scanning burial and funeral records to identify remains, and finally reburied everything they found in new caskets and vaults during rededication ceremonies carrying the blessings of the governor.

MAKING MONEY OFF CREMATION

Cremation has been the buzz word at recent NFDA conventions and cremation merchandising workshops have been standing-room only. Funeral director Tom Snyder of Washington, D.C.'s prestigious Joseph Gawler's and Sons Funeral Home—the people who embalmed JFK and the funeral parlor of choice for many Washington dignitaries—has been telling his story each year since 1992, about how Gawler went from making little or no profit on cremation to at least several hundred dollars per case by offering high-priced urns, cremation caskets, and pre-cremation visitations and services. Everyone assumed you couldn't make money off cremation, goes Snyder's line, but can you ever if you simply offer merchandise and treat cremation as you would burial.

The Cremation Association of North America (CANA) is a trade group formed in 1913, when cremation was the darling of progressive doctors, ministers, and assorted intellectuals and eccentrics pointing to the folly and waste of elaborate funerals and burial. CANA has grown to a group of 1,200 cemeteries, morticians, cremation businesses, and manufacturers, and holds its own annual convention. CANA's legal counsel is a Chicago attorney named Harvey Lapin who gives a slide show at the funeral convention each year on how to avoid getting sued for cremation transgressions. A score of class-action suits have been filed in California in the last fifteen years against crematories and the mortuaries that sent the bodies there. Several books have chronicled these crimes. (One is called *Chop Shop*.) They include rogue cremators yanking gold and silver fillings from mouths before cremating bodies; mass cremation—burning them up three, four, five, or more at a time; giving survivors commingled cremains; and the scattering of cremains any old place, like in the trash or a field, rather than a designated location, like the sea or a cemetery "scattering garden." Survivors of the wrongly cremated and wrongly dispersed have been awarded tens of millions of dollars. Lapin passes out detailed permission-to-cremate forms meant to protect morticians should survivors come back to haunt them with a lawsuit. He warns his audience to beware of the client who might claim their dearly departed didn't really want to be cremated, in spite of instructions in a will or from a relative (whom disgruntled survivors may be hostile to). Such survivors might cry emotional trauma—they had no idea cremation meant they'd be getting back all that's left of grandpa in a big baggie with a twist tie, packed in a little plastic box, itself in a cardboard box (what they expected is anyone's guess).

The granddaddy of NFDA workshops in 1994, with 200 people crammed into a sun-drenched room, was sponsored by Batesville Casket, America's giant Casketeer, headquartered in America's heartland, Batesville, Indiana. Batesville is the most profitable division of the $1.6 billion publicly traded Hillenbrand Industries. Batesville's 1995 revenue: $516 million, about half of the U.S. wholesale casket market. Hillen-brand's other death concern, Forethought Group, mentioned earlier at the Total Casket Protection booth, is a huge pay-before-you-die operation logging $141 million in 1995 revenue from about 4,000 funeral homes selling its policies. In the last eleven years, Forethought has written more than $2 billion in "preneeds," as some like to call them.

Batesville has responded to cremation's onward march by establishing a division called Options, as in options people have in the way of cremation merchandise—primarily caskets, urns, and urn vaults. By the time America's baby boomers start dying in droves around the year 2020, the casket market will have changed drastically: Many of us are expected to choose cremation. The challenge for the casketeers is to get us to buy a cremation casket. An urn and urn vault would be nice, too.

Batesville's 1994 NFDA workshop focused on these highly combustible, furnace-friendly units, made of thinner layers of wood, with no hinges or metal mattress springs. Some don't even have handles (leaving poor pallbearers without a grip.) The workshop underscores a new attitude among many funeral directors, who at first ignored cremation, then attacked it, and have now recoiled, resigned to the reality that the days of just twenty-five years ago, when more than 95 percent of deaths in America resulted in funerals and burials, are gone forever. Even the staunchest, tradition-bound mortician who believes it's a travesty of human decency to burn a body, especially without a funeral, realizes that, like it or not, cremation is here to stay. And so the adaptive attitude might be summarized thus: If you can't bury 'em, cremate 'em, because buried or burned, it ain't over until the dead person is in a casket.

THE LAST DEATH SHOW

My last funeral convention was to be in 1995. It was all becoming a little too familiar. I'd become a regular, and it was simply time to move on.

This year's show was in Orlando. It was a record-breaking year for exhibits. Dominating again were caskets and vaults and hearses. The only exhibit seeming a bit out of place was Kinko's Copies, offering customized stationery.

Bernard Yonke was back; I saw him tying up a woman's wrists as I walked by. I hadn't seen "Above and Beyond" before, so I picked up a brochure at their booth. This is a "travelers retrieval service." (The company might consider the slogan, "Don't die abroad without it.") Above and Beyond will fly your dead body home on a "private executive aircraft" from wherever you happen to die so loved ones or whoever's responsible for you don't have to deal with the hassles of paperwork and logistics if the unexpected happens. Some countries require a labyrinth of bureaucratic approval to get a body on a plane, and airlines have their own requirements, like "air trays" (a

sturdy box) for bodies and various death and health department documents. If you hadn't thought of dying away from
home, Above and Beyond's brochure reminds you: "During
your lifetime, U.S. Government statistics indicate that over 40
million Americans will die out of county, out of state, or out of
country."

Henrietta Mims, of Cherokee Casket, was back with a new
product by her side—a foot-long casket for stillborns, lined
with frilly white satin. Cherokee donates a percentage of the
sale of these units to a group researching Sudden Infant Death
Syndrome (SIDS). In back of Henrietta were baby and small
child caskets—with the biggest unit accommodating someone
five-feet-six inches tall.

Cherokee's display hit me this year with a sadness and
revulsion I hadn't yet felt at the death show. I thought of dead
children laid out in these little caskets, adorned with lace and
chiffon, and a stillborn in the tiny unit, the size of a shoe box.
And standing next to these little for-sale boxes, smiling and
greeting well-wishers, was Henrietta, a middle-aged woman
with wire rimmed glasses and styled hair, dignified in a neat
green skirt and blazer.

I shook it off and took my annual stroll through the exhibit
hall. I thought I'd seen it all: death dresses, embalming fluid the
color of cherry soda in little plastic bottles, a woman playing
corpse, a woman pasting corpse makeup on hands, and hundreds of caskets and vaults, brand spanking new and shining.

And then, this year, I came across something that topped
them all: Wilbert Burial Vault's Cameo Rose, a huge vault
glazed with a gravelly pink surface, revolving on a carpeted display three feet off the ground. "The new Wilbert Cameo Rose
burial vault," read the sign in front, "is the first vault designed
with a decidedly feminine appeal. Available January 1996."
January came around and a Cameo Rose ad appeared in our
magazine. The copy reads:

"Men call it cologne . . . Women call it perfume. Men say clothes . . . Women say fashion. Men buy mugs . . . Women buy stemware. Others call it a vault. We call it the Cameo Rose."

No one was lining up to reserve a Cameo Rose, but at the display next door a crowd of fifty gathered on fold-out seats for Wilbert's, "Vault-O-Mania," a takeoff on *Jeopardy* with a giant board flipping over answers when contestants called out, for example, "Pathology for 100" (the answer here, gangrene).

Away from the vaults by the urn booths and a company called "Kids Cope with Grief" (flanked with four giant Crayolas), was a newcomer: Afterlife Adventures of Austin. Afterlife scatters cremains at majestic dispersal locations across the country. It is apparently the first national company of the sort, with an 800-number and a promise to come fetch cremains wherever they may be. After handing over the cremains, an Afterlife rep takes it from there. What you get, says an Afterlife brochure, is "video documentation and a notarized certificate of completion" of the dispersal. Four-hundred-seventy-five dollars buys a sunrise scattering at the Grand Canyon, "by hand from the lip of the canyon." Scattering from a whale-watching boat near Pebble Beach, off the coast of Monterey Bay, costs $650. Scattering by chopper is provided "over a magnificent 400 foot waterfall" on Hawaii's Kauai. And if you'd like your human dust to be dispersed for eternity over the Rocky Mountains, Afterlife Adventures calls in the hot air balloons.

2

THE CASKETEERS

Which sex has the more to say in the selection of the casket?
I should say it would depend upon which one was dead.

—Western Undertaker, *July 1909*

Casket—1. a. A small box or chest for jewels, letters, or other things of value, itself often of valuable material and richly ornamented.

—*The Oxford English Dictionary*, second edition, 1989

Throughout human history the dead have been disposed of in many ways. They've been tossed naked into shallow graves, burned on open funeral pyres, left as sacrifice to vultures and coyotes, placed on mats and hoisted into trees, draped in shrouds and entombed in caves and cata-combs, embalmed and wrapped into mummies, slid into church vaults and mausoleum crypts, and tossed overboard and buried at sea.

In recent centuries the most common fate of bodies has been containerization: Man has seen it fit—for reasons of faith, hygiene, superstition, vanity—to put his brothers and sisters in some kind of box or boxlike contraption and lower it into the ground or slide it into a crypt.

America's container of choice in the seventeenth and eighteenth centuries was the coffin, usually a six- or eight-sided wood box, with angles like a kite, custom made for individual bodies by the local carpenter or cabinetmaker. Materials came from, where else, coffin shops and coffin warehouses. By the nineteenth century, a hodgepodge of burial containers emerged as undertaking became a distinct business and the American knack for invention went bonkers, it seems, with burial boxes for the dead. Iron, marble, stone, glass, clay, aluminum—the sky was the limit for materials used by nineteenth century coffin makers. Patents were approved for coffins made of "hydraulic" cement, "vulcanized" rubber, papier-mache, even a pottery-ware terra-cotta unit introduced in 1855. There were fusion models of cloth and wood, iron and wood, zinc, iron and glass, and one made of wood mixed with a cement made of rosin, beeswax and stone. (The cement coffin eventually metamorphosed into the burial vault.) The rich might opt for a "metallic mummy case," an iron sarcophagus (think King Tut), or a metallic coffin draped with satin and silk. The masses would settle for mass-produced wood burial cases with plain cloth covers.

By midcentury there was a new kid on the burial block, the granddaddy of them all: the casket.

A purely American invention, the popularity of the casket grew as the business of death grew with the Victorian cult of mourning. Funerals became more elaborate (at least for the well-to-do) and American merchandising ingenuity responded in kind. The fire-and-brimstone cult of gloom and doom was being supplanted by the rise of Transcendentalism and a general spirit of optimism toward death. By the 1830s, parklike cemeteries where townsfolk strolled in their Sunday best were popping up outside the cities, replacing crunched-in city graveyards bursting with bodies.

Where coffins were oblong, angling to the contours of a body, caskets were big metal rectangular boxes, long enough for any body, except the occasional seven-footer or the exceptionally obese. The casketeering undertakers felt there was a market for a new generation of burial containers, and they were right. Caskets boasted airtight sealing. Their shape, it was said, would lessen death's sting: A rectangular box offered a generic holding tank; a coffin presented an undisguised, unforgiving effigy of the body. Caskets also offered the opportunity to see the dead without opening the container lid. Early casket lids were made of two plate-glass sections divided by a name plaque; the dead were laid bare under a window for all to see. This was the container in which to see your dearly departed one last time. "Thus," explains *The History of American Funeral Directing*, the authoritative text on the matter, "the encasing of the body, the primary idea expressed in earlier receptacles, is modified toward the presentation of the dead in a receptacle designed to provide an aesthetically pleasing setting for its visually prominent and dramatically centered object of attention."

Shortly after caskets arrived, preserving bodies took on a new sense of urgency. Survivors of dead Union soldiers in the Civil War wanted fallen loved ones returned home for burial. In previous wars, the battlefield dead were often buried where they fell. This war would be different. Survivors wanted to see their loved ones one last time before the ravages of decomposition set in.

By the middle nineteenth century, some people were using metallic burial cases and caskets to ship bodies over long distances, but it didn't always stop the decomposition. An even less certain (and certainly smellier) procedure for getting a far-away body to the cemetery was smothering it in ice for as long as it took to get home. What was needed was a tried and true method of preserving the body—what was needed was embalming. At time of the Civil War, the ancient art of embalming was a fringe practice in America, conducted by "embalming surgeons" in the medical community. When the war came, a few enterprising embalming surgeons saw an opportunity and seized it. They set up shop in Washington, D.C., even established their operation near battlefields, and began embalming the war dead, reviving a practice used by the Egyptians nearly 5,000 years before. Union war heroes were embalmed and honored at open casket and-coffin public funerals, giving a national boost (at least in the north) to the up and coming undertaker trade. With embalming and caskets growing up together in this manner, America's custom of having outsiders preserve our dead and ready them for final viewing had been born.

The custom survives today as the cornerstone of the funeral industry, even as the monkey wrench of the cremation phenomenon has caused a realignment. NFDA, the funeral association, is unambiguous in its view that viewing the dead is vitally important to help survivors get over the reality of this permanent departure. A 1994 NFDA brochure called, "Someone You Loved Has Died; Some Thoughts and Suggestions about Funerals," explains:

> *One of the ways some attempt to eliminate a confrontation with death and hope to avoid the pain that loss brings, is to resist viewing the body of the deceased. They say that they wish to remember the deceased as he or she appeared alive. However, for you to view the body is an important first step toward accepting the death.*
>
> *If the death was violent or the body wasted away, our skills will be employed in such a fashion as to modify or*

erase the scars of violence or the ravages of disease. This
preparation will allow for an acceptable recall image of
the deceased.

It must be remembered that the period of the funeral,
from the first announcement of the death to the committal
service, is a declaration that a death has occurred.
Viewing, when possible, is an essential part of the affir-
mation.

Decomposition wasn't the only thing plaguing the dead.
Body-snatching "resurrectionists" were fetching fresh cadavers
from graveyards for medical students. (Dissecting bodies was
illegal in most of the country into the twentieth century.) These
enterprising ghouls, sometimes medical students themselves,
enjoyed a flourishing business; in the early 1850's, in New York
City alone, an estimated 650 bodies were stolen from graveyards. Working in groups, corpse thieves often bashed a hole in
the coffin with spades and dragged out the body. When their
shovels hit a casket, especially a powerhouse wrought-iron
unit, the jig was up for that grave, unless they took the time to
pry open the lid or lug the casket out and smash it open later.
Upping the ante for grave robbers was the coffin torpedo—little iron bombs attached to coffins set to explode when intrud-
ers started their assault on the grave. By the 1870s, someone
came up with another idea to protect the defenseless corpse—
a second container: big, unsealed wood boxes with space at the
edges for cement to be poured in for a solid sealing. These were
the precursor of the American burial vault, a variation of the
British iron grill mortsafe. Now the coveted corpse rested in
peace in a box in a box.

Despite the arrival of the casket, the coffin and burial case
jockeyed with it for predominance throughout the second half
of the nineteenth century. One of the legendary burial containers of the nineteenth century was indeed a coffin—the Fisk
Metallic Coffin. Fisks provided the all-important twin functions

of viewing and preservation. These elite iron monsters were said to be airtight, the same claim made by today's casketeers plugging the "protection" of their "hermetically sealed" metal caskets. Fisks were patented in 1848 by Almond Fisk, a New Yorker who had vowed to make a burial case that would preserve bodies after he was unable to find a container to stop his dead brother from decomposing on his journey from Mississippi, where he died, to New York, where their father waited to see his beloved son one more time before burying him in the family plot. Early Fisk units came in two mummified cuts, one following the contours of the body more closely than the other. Viewing was made easy: A cast-iron cover at the head section slid back to reveal a plate glass window directly over the dead person's face.

Fisk had made the coffin of champions: His mummified metallics won gold medals for design excellence at the American Institute Exhibition in New York and an agricultural fair in Syracuse, New York. He added to his mummy line with regular cut coffins—fitting the contours of the body—also made of iron but with an elegant imitation rosewood finish.

Fisks were expensive—from about $7 to $40—and the company accommodated custom requests, like scroll and gold leaf ornamentation. More than any burial container, the Fisk was said to be the great preserver of bodies, and undertakers had the disinterments to prove it. One came in 1877. The disinterred was someone called David Munhall, laid to rest in a Fisk Metallic in 1858. When it was opened nineteen years later, Munhall's son ". . . readily recognized his father as in a good state of preservation and commented that the clothing looked like new."

But even with a couple of gold medals racked up, the Fisk was still a coffin. The casket was the new game in town. Americans, it is said, like things big, and the casket was big, bigger than the other burial containers—and it had a great name.

JEWELRY BOX

The precise origin of the word "casket" is unknown, but variations of it had been used by the French and English to describe various boxes, crates and containers, none of them used for holding the dead. Its primary meaning by the mid-nineteenth century was a jewelry box or chest—an expensive and beautiful one—until an ingenious undertaker decided this would be the name of their new burial container. The metaphor was clear: The body was a jewel, an expired temple, deserving of protection and a final tip of the hat in a box as beautiful and dignified as the person had once been. So special was the casket that one of the first undertaker trade journals, established in 1876, was called the *Casket*.

Undertakers took great pains to pretty up their choice new merchandise. A funeral was all show and sentiment and the casket was the center of attention. An article in the July 1909 *Western Undertaker*, on "Trimming the Casket", noted:

> *"Some beautiful effects are produced by tufting the sides and bottoms of caskets with fine satins and silks. . . . The making and trimming of couch caskets has become an art of itself, and wonderful creations are being turned out by those who have become expert in this line."*

Caskets reached the fringe of America's early twentieth century burial scene, where rich eccentrics with cherished pets felt they (their pets) deserved only the best, in life and death. In 1903, an Irish setter named Dane was buried in a $75 satin-lined casket, in a "dog cemetery between White Plains and Hastings [New York]," according to *Western Undertaker*. The burial followed an elaborate $200 funeral conducted by New York undertaker Christian W. Greenwald, specialist in the embalming and burying of dogs, cats and birds.

The first casket patent application has been traced to 1849, although there may have been others a few years earlier. During the next forty years, caskets jockeyed with coffins and burial cases to be America's premier body receptacle. By the 1890s, the casket had usurped the competition; 100 years later casket companies constitute a huge chunk of the death business, and the only place you'll find coffins and burial cases in America, except for a handful of nostalgic funeral homes, are at museums or in the ground at old cemeteries, if they've not splintered into pieces (Fisks an obvious exception) and returned to the earth with their eternal cargo.

Eventually caskets spread overseas. You'll find them today in Britan and France, now that the world's largest funeral-cemetery company, Service Corporation International, owns 534 British funeral parlors and more than 1,000 in France. The London Casket Company offers "High Quality American Caskets," in a British trade journal ad, including: "the Royale, finest solid mahogany . . . Fully polished hand rubbed finish . . . finished in Bayberry Mayfield velvet. Swing bar handles and adjustable bed."

The casket merchandising revolution and the acceptance of embalming and "restorative art" would shape the death rituals of the majority of Americans into the first half of the twentieth century. We were a nation of funeral and burial and the only country with widespread embalming and expensive coffins named after a jewelry box. Embalming and caskets became as American as baseball and apple pie, although you'd be hard pressed to find anyone to admit it. (Jews have been an exception, as they usually do not embalm their dead and bury them in a simple pine coffin within twenty-four hours of death, although in recent years some Jews have accepted cremation.) To critics, America's funeral industry was the epitome of capitalism run rabid—zealous profiteering off the dead and mourning survivors. It would not have been strange to hear a global shoulder-shrugging chorus of, "Only in America." The funeral industry countered with a classic free-market defense: We're just giving the public what it wants; how else would we have survived all these years? And besides, we're carrying on ancient human rituals and customs.

Even with the rapid rise in cremation since the 1970s, the casket hangs tough as the merchandising lifeblood of the funeral industry. In 1995, American morticians bought just over 2 million caskets at a wholesale cost of more than $1.1 billion, as well as a million or so burial vaults and grave liners, discussed in the previous chapter. Consumers, in turn, bought about 1.9 million caskets in 1995, with an average retail price of $1,700.

Today's casket hard sell isn't protection from body-snatchers. Despite a steady stream of grave tamperings and stolen bones throughout the country—often by drunken, drug-crazed Satanists—it's unlikely you'll find any grave-robbing rackets these days, and the nation's medical schools have plenty of cadavers (with periodic shortages). The protection-for-the-body line is still used. Consider the Armstrong Funeral Home site on the World Wide Web, in which Canadian mortician Bruce Armstrong has a selection called, "About This Protection." In it we are introduced to his friend, Hannie, who questions the line about a casket protecting a corpse. "Who cares about this protection thing?" Hannie asks. "After all, the person is dead." Armstrong tells the reader: "I told him it was for peace of mind. If a person felt more comfortable knowing the body of the dead person was protected from the elements, like the weather and gophers and so on, that option was available to them."

It's safe to say most people don't think of gophers when buying a casket. There's really no reason for buying a casket other than you must be in one if you're to be buried or slid into a mausoleum crypt, unless you want to get out your tools and build your own, which a few people do. Many caskets are beautifully crafted pieces of work and some people—as they have for centuries—want to see their loved one for the last time in such a beautiful container. Some choose a particular casket for very personal reasons. "Most plumbers I've buried want copper caskets," explains Sumner Brashears, who was NFDA president in 1995. "They've been working with copper pipes their whole life. Everybody's got their own deal when it comes to choosing caskets."

The deal on caskets for a handful of alumni at Texas A&M University are big shiny ones in the maroon and white school colors with the alma mater logo etched inside and out. The idea for the Aggie casket came when a terminally ill alumni saw a maroon and white casket and asked the manufacturer if it could make one just like that with the Aggie logo. The company, Oak Grove International Casket of Manistee, Michigan, obliged and decided to make a few more and advertise them in the university alumni magazine. Some of the old-timer Aggies liked what they saw and phoned in their preneed order, forking out between $3,000 to $4,000, with $50 from each casket sold going into the university coffers.

Even those who think it's crazy to spend a few thousand dollars for a fancy box for a corpse often capitulate when confronted with this end-of-life decision: The dead must be buried in a container, and at most mortuaries, caskets and vaults are the only containers in town.

CREMATION THREAT TO CASKETS

The casketeers have a serious long-term problem. With cremation increasing everywhere, the threat to sales is very real— When a body is to be incinerated, who needs a casket?

The warnings have been reverberating throughout the industry. The Cremation Association of North America (CANA) waxes apocalyptic in a trade press recruitment advertisement in January 1995: "WHEN WILL THE U.S. CREMATION RATE SURPASS 40 percent? . . . SOONER THAN YOU THINK!! If the public continues to choose cremation at the current increase of only 3.4 percent a year, the U.S. cremations to deaths will surpass 40 percent BEFORE the year 2010!" This is why, the ad goes on, morticians should join the association—so they can keep up on the latest equipment, regulation, and marketing strategies. A headline in the summer 1995 newsletter of the York Group (a big casket company) warns, "Ignoring Cremation Could Be Fiscal Suicide." The Illinois Funeral Directors Association warned in its February 1995 newsletter: "Casket Use in Cremations Declines—86 percent of the 449,000 cremations in 1993 were done without a casket . . . Consumer values and buying patterns are changing. Are you adapting to meet these changes?" The Casket and Funeral Supply Association of America (CFS&A), which lists a state-by-state "Casketed Deaths" chart in a monthly newsletter, warned in late 1994 that $27 billion in casket sales will be lost to cremation through the year 2010 unless something is done—this based on a projection of 41,588,295 Americans dying from 1994 to 2010. CFS&A also laments that so few cremations take place in caskets.

The casketeers' strategy is simple: Get people who go for cremation to buy cremation caskets. Americans need to follow the example of Great Britain, the Western world's leading cremation nation, where 70 percent of the dead are cremated each year, most of them in coffins that have been the centerpiece of a funeral service. Great Britan simply ran out of burial space after World War II and started cremating people instead of burying them. But they didn't change their funeral rituals. Instead of being lowered into a grave, most deceased Brits disappear behind a curtain on a revolving platform at the end of the service. In the adjoining cremation room, they are loaded, coffin and all, into the furnace.

This doesn't happen in the United States. About 80 percent of the half-million annual cremations here occur in cardboard boxes or plywood cloth-covered caskets. These are often "direct cremations"—the no-frills, no-nothing-but-the-cremation-itself service, with cremains poured into a cardboard box and given back to survivors or a funeral director. The price of these budget cremations twenty-five years ago was as low as $175; today, direct cremation ranges from about $350 to $1,500. The conventional wisdom holds that the reason for the success of direct cremation is that most funeral directors rejected cremation when it started to gain momentum in the 1970s when California cremation societies popularized cremation and the scattering of cremains. Morticians condemned this practice as pagan and un-American, or figured it was a flaky West Coast fad that would fade away. It wasn't; America's cremation societies prospered, and a subindustry was born. The morticians had miscalculated and were paying the price with an unstoppable rising cremation rate. Many had figured cremation wasn't worth the trouble because there was no money to be made. Tom Ward, veteran casket salesman and industry consultant, puts it this way: "Funeral service made an arrogant error by assuming cremation families want low-priced containers that look cheap. Some people do want that, but not all of them!" Robert L. Waltrip, CEO of Service Corporation America, puts it this way: "Funeral directors stuck their heads in the sand and pretended cremation did not exist. I know, I was there." Waltrip is the funeral industry's entrepreneurial visionary. He started SCI with a single funeral home in Texas in 1963. While others in the industry have condemned cremation, Waltrip has acquired hundreds of mortuaries and cemeteries in the Great Britan and Australia, where cremation rates are high. "These countries have lots of cremation, and our businesses do well there," he says.

Cremation businesses also do well in the United States. The tide of rising cremation has infiltrated everywhere, even cyberspace, where you'll find dozens of cremation societies' home pages on the World Wide Web.

ELITE CARDBOARD BOX

Many casketeers and morticians understand that cremation is here to stay and they'd best learn how to turn a profit on it or face the consequences of neglecting market demand. The enemy is still the old nemesis "direct cremation," because even if you charge on the high end, there's simply nothing to sell but the cremation itself, delivery fees and a couple of cardboard boxes. A sales director notes in the Elder Davis Casket Company's fall 1995 newsletter: "We're all concerned with the trend toward cremation-in-a-cardboard-box-with-no-services." Even so, you'll find more than a few mortuaries charging $1,000 to $1,500 for this bare bones service.

Elder Davis was formed in response to the cremation phenomenon. (Check its Web Site for a more complete history.) The company asks the funeral director, in its newsletters, to sympathize with the person who's decided on cremation, rather than fret about the good old days of burial dominance, offer them lots of products, and you'll do just fine. Elder Davis specialties include inexpensive "Elderlite" pseudo-caskets, made of fiberboard and other cheap wood and wood products. They are advertised as ideal for cremation and safe for the environment. Elder Davis is a champion of Nationwide Cremation Consulting & Training, which provides cremation consultants to teach "profitable cremation solutions."

Elder Davis appears truly obsessed with keeping bodies to-be-cremated out of cardboard boxes. In late 1995, it introduced the First Step elite cardboard box mentioned earlier. An Elder Davis newsletter explains: "The First Step replaces the cardboard disposal box, the great insult to death care." The

First Step is a straight-edge rectangular box with the finish of a nondescript desk. There are no decorations, no arched lid, no handles. It could be a long tool box. Open it, and instead of bare cardboard there's "a soft, quilted Dignity Comforter and matching bolster, a mattress, and a safety liner . . . [and] a new enviroplastic latch system for security."

The idea is to give those in favor of cremation a little credit for wanting a nice container: "Would you show a cardboard box to a burial family?," writes company president Gerald Davis. "Why, then, do we underestimate and humiliate our cremation customers? That's a costly mistake." The bottom line here, of course, is profit. "It [the First Step] will move funeral directors out of the low margin direct disposal business." In a brochure above photos of three First Step models, Elder Davis reminds the mortician: "Call It Hardboard, Call It Fiberboard, You Can Even Call It Cardboard, BUT . . . Don't Call It Unsuccessful."

NO UPS CONTAINERS

The executive director of the Cremation Association of North America, Jack Springer, believes people, by and large, don't want their dead (or themselves) cremated in a cardboard box: "I don't think the public was comfortable with the idea that, 'I'm gonna look like a UPS package here to be cremated.'" Springer's been with CANA for ten years and spends a lot of time doing media interviews, during which he explains the dynamics of cremation and why it's been increasing so much, and is widely quoted in local and national newspapers. Springer understands why casketeers have been pushing cremation caskets, but thinks the First Step is a bit extreme. He mentioned how his elderly mother-in-law had arranged for her cremation and picked out a cremation casket because she didn't feel comfortable with lower-end boxes. "It was a little more expensive, but it suited her needs," Springer said. "Now, if they only had the price between the box and the real casket, she would have been stuck with, 'Well, gee, do I want to spend this money for the casket that they're going to burn up, or do I have to go in the box?'"

Death industry strategists say direct cremation wouldn't be so popular—if that's the best word—if morticians got to the cremation-minded before the body got to the crematory. The feeling is that morticians have done a lousy job dealing with America's cremation customers. As an Elder-Davis newsletter says: "Cremation customers sometimes feel that funeral homes 'punish' them for their decision to cremate."

Some mortuaries turn down cremation calls and refer them to "trade embalmers," also called "direct disposers," people licensed to embalm, pickup, and deliver bodies to crematories and funeral homes, and not much else. Why bother with cremation, say these funeral-minded morticians, if there's no money to be made and you've been reduced to middle man?

Some adopt a practical attitude toward cremation, like Sandy Stuhr, a third-generation funeral director from South Carolina, who wrote about, "serving the growing cremation market" for National Selected Morticians, a "by invitation only" association:

> "Cremation services and options must be priced at a level sufficient to recover any incurred costs. At a time when cemeteries are selling vaults, and people are choosing mausoleums rather than grave space, what once were 'big profit dollars' are dwindling rapidly. When not adequately priced, cremation can cause us to seek more income from our traditional funeral services and burial. This is neither smart nor fair, and it soon may come back to haunt us."

Some aren't so inclined to forgive cremation for rattling an industry that not too long ago took for granted that just about every dead body coming in the door was going in a casket and a vault and the ground. Some are sore that one of the core disciplines they studied in mortuary college was for naught: "Funeral directors spend two years learning to embalm and to make someone look nice, and when they come out you say, `What you do is not important; just burn it,'" explains George Foley III, a salesman for Yorktown Casket who was called on in 1994 to help launch Yorktown's line of cremation caskets, training videos and advertising strategies.

Foley and others in the vanguard of cremation merchandising say the key to making money off cremation is first selling a funeral service. The to-be-cremated, and those responsible for arrangements, are ready and willing to spend, these strategists insist. Many of us would apparently be more than happy to have a service of some kind. We also might very well be ready to buy a cremation casket rather than a cardboard box. We're all going to need urns—except for scatterers and a few zealously self-reliant types with their own containers—so why not offer them as you do caskets? The morticians must swallow their pride and treat those in favor of fire as they would those embracing the earth.

The issue for some funeral directors goes deeper than making a buck. Direct cremation, they say, denies the dead person what might be called their inalienable right as a member of the human race to an end-of-life ritual and a memorial acknowledging a life lived. Even many of the homeless get a burial and a gravemarker from governments (although some, reeling from budget cuts, are turning to cremation). What are we to make of a society where hundreds of thousands of our dead are burned and forgotten with no ceremony, no memorializing, and nothing to show but ground-up bones in a cardboard box?

Elder Davis isn't the only anti-direct cremation zealot. Joseph Dispenza, marketing director at Forest Lawn Cemetery in

Buffalo, N.Y., speaking at the 1994 convention of the Cremation Association, trashed Americans for their callous disregard of death ritual, and his colleagues for allowing it to happen:

> As Americans [we say], 'Hurry up, cremate them,' and that's the end of it. We take away all the form. We rob ourselves, our clients, and all their generations of the ability and the way to say goodbye. And that is more than a crime—it's a sin. And no one's to blame there but us. I think we have to step back and start looking at the American form of direct cremation, because we miss all ritual, all the form, all the things that make us who and what we are, by the way we're embracing it.
>
> Today we get a call, `Yes, we'll cremate mother and that's it, and we'll have a memorial service at the convenience of the family.' Death is not convenient; it's not supposed to be . . . We as professionals can not allow people who know less than we do, but think they know more, make death convenient. . . .
>
> Let me ask you a question. You get a call and somebody says, `We want to be cremated and scattered.' What do you do? You get ready, you get your boxing gloves, you figure, `I'm going to sell an urn if it kills me and it kills them. And if I don't get an urn, I'm going to sell a niche. And if I don't sell a niche, maybe I can show them a better casket or . . . ' You're going to show these people how it's done; you're the professional. . . .

Whether Dispenza is sincere or his words are a cry of anguish over the end of an era when a death almost always meant funeral and burial and the revenue that came with it is anyone's guess. The truth is some people die alone with few or no friends or family, and so no one would attend the funeral and burial. And some people tending to a dead family member may not have been particularly fond of them and have no desire to spend money or time arranging funeral and burial. When money is the prime issue, cremation is virtually always cheaper than burial.

While the Dispenzas of the industry work the humanist angle, casketeers are trying to teach morticians how to sell the cremation caskets they bring in increasing numbers each year to the funeral expos. The obsession with getting a corpse in a container isn't likely to soon fade away.

The big-ticket cremation merchandise is the incinerator-friendly cremation casket, retailing from several hundred to three thousand dollars. Next are urns and urn vaults. Many cemeteries require urn vaults, as they do burial vaults, for the same reasons: You don't want someone breaking an ankle as they step into a settled cremation grave; and although cremains are just a pile of ground-up bone, they are still human remains and should be protected in case a survivor wants them dug up and moved.

Casketeers plan to capture a piece of the cremation dollar even as they bank on old reliable metal and wood caskets. About 2.2 million people have been dying annually in recent years, and for the next decade or so about 1.8 million a year will end up in the ground or in mausoleum crypts (with a hand-ful buried at sea). So even as cremation increases, there will be a steady demand for caskets for some time.

But after the year 2011, when the first of the 76 million baby boomers—people thirty-one to fifty years old today—start moving past age sixty-five, the death rate will begin to climb steadily for about fifty years. It's clear many will choose cremation because the baby boomers are the most educated generation in history, the most environmentally conscious, the most inde-pendent thinkers, and less tied to tradition, all tendencies that suggest they're more inclined to choose cremation. The long-term question for the death industry is how many cremation-minded baby boomers (and their children) will have purchased post-death merchandise before going up in flames.

Like any industry, the casketeers and their strategists need
to move product, as they say, and are always devising innova-
tive marketing schemes. For years funeral industry consultants
have talked about the importance of arranging caskets in the
mortuary "casket selection room"—expensive ones here, wood
ones there, vaults over here, cremation room over there.
Lighting and color is also important; certain hues apparently
create mood and atmosphere more conducive to casket and
vault shopping.

Help for today's funeral director looking to boost casket
revenue is readily available. Mega-casketeer Batesville will
finance new casket selection rooms. An industry consultant
and funeral home designer named Alton Doody Jr.—a former
Ohio State University marketing professor—tells how to sell
more caskets in general and more expensive caskets in particular in his 1994 book, *Reinventing Funeral Service*. Doody
wants caskets stripped of factory model numbers and replaced
with dignified names. He suggests metal elites be knighted
"Monarch" or "Congressional," while bottom-of-the-barrel
wood poplars can settle for "Huntley" or perhaps "Fairlane."
He is very serious. He spent months touring casket selection
rooms throughout the country and researching the industry
before writing his book. What Doody doesn't suggest is what
seems like the obvious name for a casket, regardless of price
and quality: Name it for the poor soul going inside, as was the
case with nineteenth century plate-glass caskets.

SELLING CREMATION FAMILIES VIDEO

To help morticians sell cremation merchandise, the major casketeers have produced training videos. Batesville's is called,

"Arranging Cremation Services." At the start, the narrator concedes:

> *"For the past two decades, cremation has presented a strong challenge to funeral service. While funeral preferences have changed, the funeral industry has not kept pace with those changes. Industry perceptions of cremation consumers are often inaccurate, illustrating a better need for better communication between funeral arrangers and family."*

The video stresses the importance of selling a service to a family cremating their dead. If you've hooked them on a service, the sky's the limit. The body must be embalmed, dressed, dabbed with cosmetics. Hair should be done. Bodies must be in a casket in a visitation room for survivors to pay final respects. An obituary should go in the newspaper. A bevy of trimmings, from prayer cards to canned music, can be sold.

The options video centers on a skit with a fictitious middle-aged son and daughter making plans with Jay Allen, a fictitious funeral director, for their recently expired mother, who "had talked about being cremated" but left no instructions.

Jay is a somewhat handsome man of about thirty-five in a dark suit with neatly combed black hair. He speaks in a slow, earnest manner. He never smiles, never frowns. He is emotionally neutral. The opening scene shows him seated at a desk taking a call from Mark Paterson. Mark's mother just died and he wants to know what Jay offers in the way of cremation. Jay says they have three services: "Cremation with visitation and service, includes a family gathering and ceremony, for $2,450. A cremation with memorial service, in our chapel, is $1,795. And direct cremation, with no services, is $1,070. I'd be very interested in meeting with you to discuss our services and prices in more detail. Mark, could you possibly come to the funeral home this afternoon?"

Mark isn't sure. His sister, Susan, is flying in from Boston (they are in Tampa), and he's going to the airport to pick her up.

The scene is frozen. "How Would You Respond?" appears. Viewers—presumably the only people watching this are funeral directors—are asked to hit pause and take a few minutes to discuss it.

The action restarts. Jay responds, "Well, that's fine, Mark. Just a couple of thoughts. If it would help, we could send a driver to the airport for your sister, and if you choose our funeral home, we'll pick your mother up from the hospital immediately and bring her here, where we'll provide some basic preparation and care."

Mark's voice is sad, noncommittal. "Well, Okay, maybe we could meet around three o'clock. I can pick up my sister, since she's expecting me."

Mark is hooked. Jay tells him to bring his mother's vital statistics—date of birth, Social Security Number, mother's maiden name—and ends the conversation saying, "We request you bring in clothing, either this afternoon or at a later date."

Mark agrees and scene one ends. The narrator returns. She is pretty, about forty, with heavy lipstick and strawberry blond bangs, and wearing a sharp blue blazer. "Most importantly," she says, "when asked about the price of cremation, the arranger did not assume direct cremation. He remained objective and offered information about all cremation options. He engaged the caller in an open dialogue. He was interested in who had died and the family situation. He let the family know he wanted the service and conveyed a willingness to serve the family. Consumers are much more likely to select a firm who really wants the business. By arranging a meeting as quickly as possible, the arranger avoided the necessity of asking for permission to embalm over the telephone. It's too easy for the caller to decline embalming as unnecessary, and the opportunity for services may be gone. Remember, the choice to embalm can be discussed further during the arrangement conference. The arranger took the opportunity to explain the personal nature of the services, his competitive strength, and thus provided the motivation for the caller to make the decision in his favor."

Another smart thing Jay did, in terms of bringing in revenue, was asking for clothing. "Many funeral directors find the request for clothing plants a seed for visitation and service," the narrator explains. "It opens the door for seeing the person again, and shows the importance you place on dignity for the deceased."

Jay immediately gave prices over the phone because under the federal Funeral Rule he has to. About seventy-five funeral homes have been fined about $2 million since the late 1980s by the Federal Trade Commission for not giving out prices over the phone, not giving price lists at the funeral home, not asking for permission to embalm, and other infringements. Morticians are reminded by their associations that FTC agents posing as funeral shoppers call and visit funeral homes randomly asking for prices. The permission to embalm requirement stems from the old days when many funeral directors embalmed all their bodies because virtually everyone had a funeral and burial; you can't have an evening or two of viewing with another day for the funeral unless the corpse is preserved. This automatic embalming was one of the great ripoffs of the old days, according to people fighting the funeral industry in two decades of congressional hearings. Now that morticians are supposed to get permission to embalm, Batesville's video suggests they're more likely to get it in person. This explains the narrator's note that Jay did good by gliding over the "permission to embalm" question with Mark.

With pause button released, the camera rolls and Jay, Mark, and his sister, Susan, are seated at a round wood table at the funeral home. Jay shows them a "general price list" and says: "We need to choose several containers. One for the cremation itself, and an urn for the cremated remains. Before we begin, do you have any immediate questions or concerns?"

Susan offers immediate resistance: "Well, we're not interested in an elaborate service. I mean, Mom just retired, so she didn't know very many people. So I don't think we'll need a visitation or anything."

"How Would You Respond?" returns to the screen. The scene is frozen on Susan's serious face. The camera rolls and Jay responds, "Well, that's fine. I'm sure we can arrange something simple that will allow you to pay tribute to your mother without being elaborate. Why don't I explain all of your options so we can arrange something that will meet your needs. Basically, there are four types of cremation services; visitation and service, private viewing and service, private viewing only, or a memorial service. A visitation and service includes a gathering of family and friends, to provide comfort and support for one another. A visitation is usually open to anyone who wishes to attend. The service can be religious or contemporary, or a combination of both. In a contemporary service, family and friends become more active participants by sharing their memories and feelings. For some families, this makes the ceremony a lot more meaningful. The private viewing and service is similar, with the exception that the viewing is only open to family members and close friends you request."

Before explaining "private viewing only"—where the family gets a few minutes with the body before it's delivered to the crematory—or the bodiless "memorial service," Jay first reminds Mark and Susan that, "many people find viewing to be helpful by providing a positive and peaceful image of the person that you can add to your memories of their lifetime. It also provides a chance to say goodbye."

Now Jay explains options three and four: "A private viewing only is for those who do not want a formal service but want to see the person for the last time and say their goodbyes. And lastly, a memorial service is another way of paying tribute, and it is usually held here at the funeral home. This enables our staff to arrange and oversee the many details of the service. Many people choose to have the cremated remains present in an urn to provide a focal point for the service. Any type of service can be individualized, with musical selections or readings or displays of your mother's life (Susan is nodding her head in earnest understanding), her occupation, or her interests. We encourage you to express any ideas that will help us to arrange a more meaningful and personalized service. Do any of these services seem appropriate to you?"

Mark responds: "Well, I think we should do something for Mom, maybe, like a small private service. I know they have, at the condominium, in the clubhouse, I know they've done it before."

Again, "How Would You Respond?"

An obstacle has been thrown at Jay. If the service is held outside the funeral home, it's likely to be a bodiless memorial service. There go the casket sale and facility charges.

Not to worry.

"Sure, that can be arranged," says Jay. "Or, if you care to hold the services here, we can help you to arrange and oversee the details of the service. Also, the casket can be present at the service, either open or closed, which adds significance and meaning to the service. Our facilities really are excellent for a small gathering. It's very comfortable with plenty of space, and it has a break room."

Perhaps it was the break room, for Jay's response seems to have killed Mark's clubhouse idea. Susan asks, "What are your charges for the service?" Jay tells her it's $390 and Susan responds: "And I'm sure well worth it. I'd much rather have the service here than have to worry about the details at the condo."

Jay takes this as a yes. "Fine. Are there many people who might want to attend? Friends of your mother, or yours. Was she involved in any clubs or organizations?"

Mark says: "Actually, she was in the bridge club here in town, and, you know, some of those people might like to come.

And then, also, a few of my friends got to know her pretty well. I think they'd like to attend." Susan nods her head in agreement.

Jay offers to publish an obituary in the local newspaper, and Susan says, "I'm really glad you mentioned that. I think we need to put it in the newspaper. You know, come to think of it, Mom really did make friends quickly."

Jay asks, "Would you like us to have your mother ready so that you can see her?"

Susan: "I'd like to see Mom again."

Jay: "So we can begin embalming and preparation?"

Sluggishly Mark says, "Yeah, I agree. I think we should, I think that's the way to go."

Jay: "Now, you might like to come an hour early to the service for some private time with your mother. Would you prefer for the casket to be left open for the others to say their good-byes?"

Susan says no, shut it after she and Mark say goodbye.

Jay suggests a "memorial table of mementos," and Susan remembers that, "Mom's needle point work was great. I'd really like that to be a part of the service. I think Mark and I can gather that together."

"Very good," says Jay. "Also, during the ceremony you're welcome to say a few words. Are there any readings or poems that have special meaning to either of you or your mother?"

Susan: "Yeah, there was a poem by Emily Dickinson that Mom loved. But, you know, I don't think I could do it. Do you think you could do it, Mark?"

"Yes, I think I'd like to do that," says Mark, and Jay finishes with, "I think you'll both remember the service for a long time."

The narrator suddenly pops in front of the camera: "The family selected a private viewing and service with casket present because the arranger offered the option to them and explained why those services would be helpful."

Scene three has Jay going over casket prices with Mark and Susan.

"Next," begins Jay, "we should select the casket or container for the viewing and cremation . . . traditional caskets, cremation caskets, or alternative containers. Some people prefer the design and ornamentation of traditional caskets. Any of our eight hardwood caskets may be used for cremation. They range in price from $5,900 to $1,195. Cremation caskets are simpler in design and are constructed specifically for cremation. They contain a minimal amount of metals and ornamentation. Now, we have a separate selection room in our funeral home for cremation products, with five cremation caskets on display, ranging in price from $2,695 to $395. An alternative container is also available, which is made of cardboard. Would you prefer to see the traditional caskets, or those designed specifically for cremation?"

Susan takes the lead again: "We want to stay with something simple, so let's look at the cremation caskets."

The action moves to the cremation merchandise room, where Jay informs Mark and Susan about Batesville's tree-planting program: "The cherry is constructed of one of the finest woods available. Our medium price selection is the oak, obviously a popular selection. The poplar and the pine offer choices at lower prices, and the minimum veneer casket has a wood frame with a thin veneer covering. For all of these caskets, we participate in a program called the Living Memorial. At our request, the manufacturer of these caskets will arrange for a tree to be planted in a national forest, as a living memorial to the person who has died. Is there a type of wood that might be more suitable? Did your mother have any personal favorites?"

"Yes," says Susan, "she was really proud of that cherry dining room set." She looks at Mark, "Do you think that would be appropriate?"

Mark agrees: "You know, I think the cherry will be fine."

A film clip of a man planting a small pine tree in a forest appears. A voice over explains: "Many cremation-oriented consumers are concerned about environmental issues and appreciate this contribution to reforestation," and without pause adds, "We recommend showing the cardboard container in the cremation selection room. Consumers who want the minimum container should see what they're selecting."

Jay is back to orchestrate "the final selection"—choosing an urn.

"These are cast-bronze urns, made of the highest quality of sculptured bronze. They are cast using the lost wax method—the same process used creating bronze statues, so they are perfect artwork for the home . . . The hardwood urns range from mahogany, at the highest quality, to oak and poplar, at more basic prices. The mahogany and cherry urns are hand-crafted in highly detailed designs . . . We offer several memento boxes, which can hold cremated remains or personal mementos, such as jewelry and other keepsakes. These two urns are crafted in solid cherry, if you'd like to select an urn to complement the cherry casket . . ."

Jay moves on to marble urns, then low-end "sheet bronze" units and wraps it up by asking the brother and sister if they have a preference.

Mark doesn't know: "We haven't really discussed what we want to do with the ashes." Susan asks, "What can we do with the ashes?" Jay: "The urn can be buried at a cemetery in a family plot, if you have one. Or in an urn garden. It can be placed in a niche at the cemetery or kept in the home." (He doesn't mention scattering, which might cost an urn sale.)

Susan has an idea: "Why don't we bury the ashes in the cemetery next to Dad. Can that be arranged?"

"Oh," says Jay, "we can call the cemetery right away and find out. Should we go ahead and select the urn, or wait until we hear back from the cemetery?"

Not so fast, says a suddenly curious Mark: "Well, wait a

minute; can all these urns be buried?" You bet, says Jay: "Oh yes, any urn can be buried. The cemetery does, however, require an urn vault, which we can provide."

Speaking on behalf of his sister, Mark concludes the skit with, "I think we really like the cherry."

Jay has sold the Patersons a service and visitation for $2,345; an embalming, which averages about $400; the top-of-the-line cremation casket, for $2,695; an expensive cherry urn; an urn vault; an obituary placement; and who knows what other trimmings the script-writer might have dreamed up. All this to a "cremation family," which will get a bill over $5,000.

The narrator comes back to wrap things up, first with a word on scattering: "When a family chooses to scatter, you might encourage them to establish a permanent memorial as a way of remembering their loved ones. They might also keep a small amount of cremated remains in case they change their mind at a later date." And then a reminder of the bottom line: "We hope the techniques we offered help you to better service cremation oriented families, and at the same time, they can mean improved profitability for your firm. Those who choose cremation care about their loved ones. Often they're not aware of their options or how helpful your services can be. Your responsibility is to make them aware . . ."

The York Group's cremation division, Traditions by York, also produced a training video, also using skits and an attractive female narrator—this one a little younger and prettier than Batesville's, with dark hair and eyes.

"Notice that our funeral director was careful to explain the merchandise before offering it," she says after a scene from a preneed conference with a "Mr. and Mrs. Jones" and their daughter. "Also note that when Mrs. Jones indicated she didn't want to spend $4,495 for a casket, the funeral director did not quickly flip to the lowest price offerings. He did not judge Mrs. Jones' comment about not wanting to spend a lot of money.

Mrs. Jones' perception of a lot of money—if someone asked for the best you have, would you start with a cardboard box? Well, certainly not. Neither should you prejudge the person who does not want to spend a lot of money." The video has an hour of such play-acting and analysis.

The Traditions line of "cremation containers" are subcontracted to Elder Davis. These low-end units are identified by the Elder Davis patented acronym, C*O*P*E—*Cremation Oriented Product Engineered*. Browsing through the Traditions flip-chart folder—compiled before the creation of the First Step elite cardboard box - you'll find the "Carter" hardwood poplar unit, with satin finish and crepe interior, looking close enough to a casket, as does the "Glenwood" fiberboard, with "optically embossed oak veneer" and "pebble crepe interior." It's not until you flip to the straight-edged "Minimum" flannel-covered fiberboard rectangular box (with pillow and mattress), and the bottom of the barrel "corrugated box" (wholesaling for about $28) that you see these are indeed "alternatives" to the real thing.

HEAVY METAL CREMATION

The casket sale is so important some casketeers push for cremation in metal caskets, and some crematories oblige. The first caskets were metal, and today about 85 percent of caskets sold each year are copper, bronze, or steel. As absurd and dangerous as it may seem to slide a giant metal box with a body inside into a cremation furnace, it happens about 3,000 times a year, according to the cremation association's container surveys. One argument for metal casket cremation: Pure cremains. When the cremation is finished, the bones rest un-commingled on the metal casket mattress—no casket ash, hinges, nails, or other debris mixed in with the bones.

Most of the 4,000 bodies arriving annually at the crematory at Rosehill and Rosedale Cemetery in Linden, New Jersey, are in boxes, plastic containers, and cheap caskets, as is the case at most of the country's crematories. But sometimes a metal unit rolls in. Rosehill's crematory operator, a man identifying himself to me only as John, said he didn't look forward to cremating metals because it takes so long. First they must be stripped of plastic and metal ornamentation. Then the "hermetically sealed" metal lid must be clipped open so the flames can engulf the corpse. Another inconvenience: The burning shell gets extremely hot. This makes it risky to reposition the body, necessary sometimes if body parts aren't burning adequately. The operator must simply wait for the body to burn, however long it takes.

The aftermath of a metal-casket cremation is a burned-out shell that takes ten hours to cool. This means these cremations must be scheduled at the end of the day so they can cool overnight. Before the shell can be discarded, the metal mattress must be extracted so the bones can be swept off. The book *Cremation*, written in 1968, reported that, "Some metal coffins with a high melting point must be broken up with a sledge hammer" after a cremation.

Finally, the charred metal casket shell must be disposed of. Rosehill stores them in a garage until space runs out, at which time a refuse company hauls them off as recyclable metal.

A crematory in Tijuana, Mexico, according to the cremation association, uses a hybrid wood-metal casket that could serve as a model for crematories around the world. The bottom is metal and the rest is wood. This lets the body burn cleanly with the bones laid out on the metal sheet. No mattress to extract; no klunky shell to drag out.

Aurora Casket is one of the largest casket manufacturers in the U.S. It specializes in metal units. Its vice president of marketing, Dick Smith, argued during a "point-counter-point" at the cremation association's 1994 convention that taking metals out of the cremation arena was unfair because people may want the body of a loved one in metal for personal reasons.

"It's been proven many, many times that one of the major factors in casket selection is eye appeal," Smith told the crowd. "To me, translated, this means 'Does it look like Mom or Dad?' When you go in the selection room with people, that's what they're looking for, primarily. Yes, money comes into it and all that sort of thing, but they want something that looks like mom or dad. If the pink metal casket over here looks like mom, should we tell them, 'Sorry, folks, you can't use the pink metal casket, you have to use the one over here that doesn't quite look like mom?' So, again, should we, as often happens today, restrict choices?"

Whether passed-away mother looks better in pink metal or an earthy oakwood brown, what's important is not losing the casket sale.

A rental casket is fine for some. They are usually wood with a cardboard box insert removed after viewing. York's "Norwood Alternative" rental unit has a "fiberboard cremation container" inside. At Rutherford Funeral Homes and Crematories in Columbus, Ohio, $195 will rent you a "cloth-covered particle board" casket. On the high end, $995 rents a stainless steel unit. Buying them would cost $500 and $2,300, respectively. (1994 prices.)

For some in the funeral industry, there's a yearning for a simpler time when a death virtually guaranteed a funeral and burial. Michael Kubasek, a mortician in Burbank, California, wrote *Cremation and the Funeral Director: Successfully Meeting the Challenge in 1990*. The book is sold by NFDA, and like the casketeers' videos, offers strategies for making profits off cremation.

Kubasek, who says he provides a funeral procession to the crematory even if survivors haven't requested it, speaks at the death conventions on cremation liability. In 1995 Kubasek told a gathering of the Ohio Funeral Directors Association that, "The cremation consumer has been the most neglected and maligned consumer in the past twenty years." In spite of this, there's always the chance of bringing the cremation-minded back into the burial camp. Kubasek says he's pulled off such conversions, including one he writes about in his book:

> One day the daughter of an employee came to visit with her mother. During a brief chat with her, she remarked that, when she dies, she wants to be cremated. I asked why, and she responded that she didn't want to be buried because she didn't want 'bugs and other things to do things to my body.' She appeared to have strong feelings about the subject, but at the same time seemed to lack knowledge regarding certain funeral practices and merchandise. For example, she was unaware that protective metal caskets provide air and water seals. I briefly described these caskets and explained how [they] work. She was fascinated by this information and reversed her earlier preference for cremation. This example illustrates the need for us to determine why someone desires cremation. It is fair to assume, from my experience, that many persons choose cremation out of lack of knowledge and resultant misconceptions.

This longing for earth burial and the casket sale goes back to the early days of the dismal trade, as the business of undertaking was sometimes called. In 1914, the Belmont Casket Manufacturing Company of Bellaire, Ohio, ran a full-page ad in the *Embalmer's Monthly* trade journal. Belmont specialized in "Lead-Coated-Steel" caskets. "We have been surrounded so comfortably by flimsy wood caskets for so long that we have completely lost sight of the purpose of the casket," goes the ad copy. A few lines later came this decree: "You are under obligation to show each patron the danger of burial in the ground.

Explain what takes place in a water-soaked grave and urge the selection of a casket that will give as much protection as possible."

Today, the protection hard sell is still around. Yes, dead is dead, but some morticians will tell you that folks feel a sense of relief knowing loved ones are locked up good and tight in a big solid casket in a big solid vault.

3

THE CREMATIONISTS

The Post-Master General has ruled that cremated remains may be sent through the mail as fourth-class matter.

—The Western Undertaker, *October 1903*

The burning of dead humans by fellow humans has been practiced for millennia. Australian aborigines were thought to be cremating their dead 20,000 years ago. Scandinavians were cremating in the Bronze Age, Palestinians in the Iron Age. The Babylonians cremated their dead, as did the Greeks and Romans. Japan, today with a 97 percent cremation rate, began cremating its dead in the eighth century.

With the fall of the Roman Empire and the rise of Christianity, burial became the disposal method of choice in the Western world from about the Fifth Century A.D. until the last quarter of the nineteenth century, when the cremation furnace was invented and the era of modern cremation was born. Before the cremation furnace, bodies (and the occasional unfortunate soul burned at the stake) were incinerated outside.

Doctors are more responsible than anyone for cremation's reemergence in the modern world. They blamed bloated burial grounds for epidemics and disease and saw cremation as the natural and sensible solution to the problem. Cremation also became a cause célèbre for socialists and leftist clergy repulsed by extravagant funerals and gaudy cemetery monuments. All indeed was vanity for the capitalists, and they perversely insisted on bringing it with them to the grave. It was obscene, they protested, to spend so much money on the dead when so many of the living lived in poverty and squalor. Cremation, more so than death itself, could be the Great Equalizer, as rich and poor alike would face the same fiery end.

Transcendentalists liked to think of cremation as a magnificent release of the spirit from a corrupted earthly shell. Eccentrics saw cremation as a way of making an unforgettable final impression: Funeral and burial were common; having your body torched was outrageous, spectacular, scandalous.

On the fringe were what might be called extreme utilitarians, who argued that cremation fires could be harnessed for power, and bones from cremated bodies used as fertilizer. "If we are quite satisfied a corpse is simply so much fat, so much water, ammonia, lime and so forth, and nothing else," wrote British funeral expert Bertram Puckle in 1926, summarizing the logic of these practical-minded cremation advocates, "what possible harm can there be in separating such parts from the whole as would be usefully employed for manufacture or agricultural purposes?"

The man who built America's first cremation furnace, in 1876, and conducted the country's first enclosed cremation in it, was an eighty-year-old doctor from Washington, Pennsylvania, F. Julius Le Moyne. Before Le Moyne, there'd been a smattering of outdoor cremations on funeral pyres—a pile of wood stacked high, usually set ablaze with leaves and kindling, common in India and other countries with Hindu and Buddhist populations. The most notable of America's early cremations was that of Colonel Henry Laurens in 1792. Colonel Laurens apparently wanted to make a statement on the folly of burial after his daughter was almost buried alive. His body was "enfolded in twelve yards of tow-cloth and burned," according to the book *Death to Dust: What Happens to Dead Bodies?* About the time of Laurens' cremation, people were pointing fingers at jam-packed graveyards in New York, New Haven, Cincinnati, and other cities as the source of yellow fever epidemics. By the 1830s, cities began dealing with the problem by laying out rural cemeteries on the outskirts of town, and the era of beautifully landscaped and decorated burial grounds had arrived. Throughout this rural cemetery movement, cremation lingered at the fringe—a cremation here, a cremation there, often followed by charges of blasphemy from the faithful. Burning bodies brought to mind human sacrifice, pagan rites. By the late nineteenth century, however, "Cremationists," as they called themselves, were organized and serious. Cremation furnaces were being built, many at cemeteries, and the faithful were not amused.

CATHOLIC CHURCH NOT PLEASED

The Roman Catholic Church took the lead opposing the modern cremation movement. Christians, like Jews and Muslims, were supposed to bury their dead. Cremation was bad, said the Church, for a variety of reasons. Foremost, for all intents and purposes it ruined your chance of Judgment Day resurrection. At the end of time, God would judge the living and the dead. Everyone would be resurrected and sentenced to Hell or elevated to Heaven (perhaps with some time in purgatory). In a couple of hours, cremation annihilated the body and left a pile of bones. Needless to say, it was hard to imagine a pile of bones reformulating into a now-vaporized body for an end-of-the-world day of reckoning. A body in the ground was the representation of the person to be resurrected; it was still the temple of the soul, despite its current incarnation as corpse. What it had been it would become once more come that fateful day. It apparently didn't matter that a body buried in consecrated ground would become a skeleton, which would crumble to—what else?—a pile of bones. Of course this would take a decade or two, or, with a good embalming, much longer, maybe even a century or two. Here, then, was the rub: The dead from centuries past were no more than dust in the wind, as the song goes, but they got there through what you might call righteous decomposition.

Another reason Catholics balked at cremation: Jesus Christ. Jesus may not have been buried—he was entombed—but what mattered was that his body wasn't annihilated by flames. Cremation would have made his resurrection prohibitive, if not impossible.

Another reason the Catholic Church gave an unambiguous thumbs down to cremation: memories of tormentors and persecutors. In the early centuries A.D., Christian martyrs were often burned. Their killers taunted the faithful by asking how their God planned to resurrect bones. To pour salt in the wound, heathens would divvy up the bones and scatter them miles apart.

The Catholic Church had its own revenge ritual for dead heretics mistakenly buried in consecrated ground. The punishment, sure enough, was cremation. In the Middle Ages, the Church would go to the trouble of digging up and burning up the remains of misplaced sinners. One such occasion happened in 1425 in Lutterworth, England. Heretic John Wyckliffe had been dead for forty-one years. Somehow he ended up in a Catholic burial ground. The authorities found out, exhumed his bones, burned them, and dumped the ashes in a river.

The bottom line many Catholics kept returning to was the "p" word—cremation was pagan. All one had to do was look at the past. Roman gladiators clashed as funeral pyres burned. Vikings strapped dead warriors onto sea vessels before setting them ablaze and casting them off on their final voyage. The Greeks burned fallen comrades on the battlefield so the enemy couldn't desecrate them. Ancient kings were cremated after commoners spent days celebrating their passage to the next realm, with the ceremony culminating in the portioning out of his bones after they were washed with milk or wine and sprinkled with perfume or mixed with clay.

This was not model Christian behavior.

Christians were to be buried in consecrated ground—the Catholic burial ground. A community of the faithful in death, their final responsibility to the Creator was to lie waiting for Judgment Day together. Writing in the July 1917 *Western Undertaker*, someone identified only as Father O'Neill of St. Paul, Minnesota, explained:

> *"The church has always opposed cremation or burning the bodies of the dead. She holds that it is unseemly that the human body, once the living temple of God, the instrument of heavenly virtue, sanctified so often by the sacrament, should finally be subject to a treatment at which filial piety and friendship revolts against. Whenever cremation is introduced, it is invariably the outgrowth of materialism and irreligion."*

Cremation was condemned throughout the twentieth century in books, articles, homilies at masses, addresses at conventions, and no doubt in private conversations between the faithful and their clergy. Published in 1965, *Cremation: Is It*

Christian? attacked cremation "from the standpoint of evangelical theology and biblical realism." This was just two years after the Catholic Church had lifted its ban on cremation. Ban or no ban, many of the faithful weren't—and still aren't—buying this liberal policy covering their lifeless bodies.

The Church's formal ban on cremation had been in effect for just seventy-seven years. Through the centuries, Rome had issued decrees warning the faithful against cremation, but it apparently never banned it outright until 1886. During the crusades, the Church banned the boiling of bones from disemboweled bodies. Christian soldiers did this so they didn't have to carry home the bodies of fallen comrades intact; it was easier to literally boil them down to their bones, load them into sacks and cart them home. They also plucked out and preserved an occasional heart for home burial. (All this boiling didn't settle well with Pope Boniface VIII, who banned the practice in 1300.)

I first heard of Christian boiling practices from the Monsignor Nunzio Defoe, who's been running a Catholic cemetery and crematory near Vancouver, British Columbia, since the early 1970s. Monsignor Defoe is the Catholic Church's cremation point man for the North American cemetery industry. He has served on the boards of the U.S. national cemetery and cremation associations mentioned in earlier chapters, served a term as president of the United States National Catholic Cemetery Conference and is secretary for a cremation association in British Columbia. You'll see Monsignor Defoe each year at the cemetery and cremation conventions (I haven't seen him at the funeral show), often donning dark glasses as he mingles with the crowd during receptions. Through the years, the Reverend Defoe has delivered many speeches at the conventions, drawing on scholarly papers he's written on cremation to set the record straight about where the Catholic Church stands. Plenty of people still think Rome gives a resounding no to cremation, when the

party line is that Rome gives an unenthusiastic okay to cremation, as long as it isn't being performed in defiance of Church
teachings. The bottom line is the Catholic Church would
rather see its members buried or entombed in a Catholic burying ground but will not condemn you if you must be cremated.

Monsignor Defoe knows the historic details of cremation.
After taking the podium at the 1994 Cremation Association of
North America convention, he corrected a speaker who had
mistakenly referred to the Church's banning of cremation
when it was actually the banning of boiling, a fine but important distinction the Monsignor felt the people in the cremation
business should know. Monsignor Defoe sits on the consumer
complaint board of the cemetery association, and has no
patience for sales tactics used by "memorial counselors" pitch-
ing graves to the elderly. (The badgering of senior citizens on
the phone by cemetery telemarketers is one of Monsignor
Defoe's pet peeves, and he reminds me it's against the law in
Canada.) As one of North America's cremation experts, the
Monsignor has been deposed or called as an expert in three
California court cases involving rogue cremation operations.
The most recent case came in the summer of 1995 when
Monsignor Defoe traveled to Sebastopol, California, to share
his knowledge of cremation for a case involving a crematory
charged with cremating bodies together. The allegations sur-
faced after someone found something in the cremains of a
loved one that could not possibly have been theirs—someone
else's teeth.

THE CREMATION FURNACE ARRIVES

The pivotal event in the modern practice of burning the dead
indoors came in 1873. That year an Italian professor of anato-
my, Ludovico Brunetti, displayed the first cremation furnace at

a medical exposition in Vienna. In attendance was Queen Victoria's surgeon, Sir Henry Thompson. Sir Henry was impressed with Brunetti's remarkable invention and how cremation might help with the battle against various diseases, which many believed were caused, at least in part, from dead bodies. A year later he founded the Cremation Society of England.

Word of the new technology spread through Europe and the United States. Cremation was already a topic in the U.S. medical community—the *Boston Medical & Surgical Journal* published an article in 1870 titled, "Burning the Bodies of the Dead"—and by 1876, the U.S. had its first cremation furnace. By 1878 Germany had one; in 1880 cremationists in Paris founded a group called Propagation of Cremation; in 1884 cremation companies were formed in New York and Cincinnati; by 1886 the International Cremation Congress was established in Gotha, Germany.

Cremation was cutting edge technology and a rallying point for progressive men of science and medicine. It challenged the rigid death dictates of the Catholic Church. Those promoting cremation could site a dozen reasons why it was better than burial, including incidentals—like not worrying about getting soaked at a rainy graveside service, as the cremation, of course, occurred inside—as well as serious health and philosophical arguments. Articles on cremation began showing up in scholarly journals. By the mid-1880s, American cremationists had their own journals. One of the first, *The Modern Crematist*, was founded in 1886 by M. L. Davis, who operated a crematory in Lancaster, Pennsylvania. Another, *Urn: A Monthly Journal Devoted to the Interests of Cremation*, started in 1892, played cousin to the undertaker's *Casket* journal.

With cremation furnaces popping up throughout the United States and Europe, the Catholic Church was not pleased and officially banned cremation in 1886. The ban was lifted in 1963 during Vatican II, at least in part because Asians, who often practice cremation, were flocking to the Church; Rome apparently didn't want to miss this opportunity for a mass infusion of converts, and compromised.

AMERICAN CREMATION VISIONARY

Word of Europe's first cremation furnace spread quickly to the United States. The man who took up the mantle was the recently turned octogenarian Dr. F. Julius Le Moyne. Le Moyne had a long career as activist and reformer. He'd been an abolitionist and ran for vice president on the Liberty Party ticket in the 1840s. Shortly after Brunetti introduced his furnace in Vienna, Le Moyne decided to build one for himself. He wanted to make a final contribution to humanity by showing the country the sensible way to dispose of one's body—going up in smoke. Le Moyne's first client was to be Le Moyne.

His furnace was a one-story brick structure, thirty feet long, twenty feet high, with a little reception room. Le Moyne described it as a "fire-clay retort such as is used in the manufacture of illuminating gas, but somewhat of a different shape, heated to a red heat before the body is introduced." The body was to be covered with a wet cloth and saturated with "a solution of sulphate of alumine (common alum), which even when burned, retains its form and prevents any part of the corpse from being seen until the bony skeleton begins to crumble down." Le Moyne suggested the crumbled bones could be, "placed for preservation in a one gallon salt-mouthed druggist's bottle, with large ground stopper, into which a photograph of the deceased, with appropriate record, can be placed before introducing the remains." The idea was to have some kind of memorial for the world to see, even if it was a pile of bones in a jug rather than a tombstone over a body in a casket. The ancients had favored urns; Le Moyne, a practical man with apparently simple tastes, favored the drugstore bottle. "This bottle," he suggested, "can be placed in the columbarium of the crematory, kept among the cherished memorials of the family of the deceased, or placed besides other remains previously buried in cemeteries or graveyards."

Le Moyne ended up cremating two people before he died in 1878. The man with the claim to fame of being America's first indoor crematee was an eccentric follower of the religion of theosophy, Joseph Henry Louis, also called the Baron de Palm. (Theosophists believed in reincarnation.) The Baron's cremation made news. This was a first for America. The press was covering it. Doctors and health officials were overseeing it. Le Moyne was making history. (His furnace stands today in its original location at the Le Moyne Museum.)

The Baron's body was taken from a mausoleum crypt in Brooklyn's Lutheran Cemetery to Jersey City and shipped by rail to Pittsburgh. From there it traveled another thiry miles to Le Moyne's crematory. *The New York Times* had covered the Baron's funeral and was now covering his cremation. The *Times* reporter wrote about the transfer of the Baron's body as if writing ad copy for the makers of embalming fluid: "The features of the deceased were found to be remarkably well-preserved, and appeared as lifelike as when first entombed, showing the wonderful preservative properties of the acids and poisons used in the process of embalming," he wrote in an article on December 6, 1876. As far the Baron's cremation, technically there were no problems but all was not well. Townspeople threatened to destroy the furnace because there'd been no religious service. "The first cremation had been judged a circus of infidels, just as conservatives had predicted," according to *The Last Great Necessity*, a book on the history of American cemeteries. The burning of bodies just didn't sit well with many God-fearing folks, especially when it was in their backyard. An early cremation episode in England ended in near violence when a British mob stopped an eighty-four-year-old cremation fanatic, Dr. William Price, from cremating a five-month-old baby in a "tub of paraffin," according to one account, in front of worshipers leaving a Sunday evening church service. The faithful chased Price home, the story goes, and his daughter held them off with a shotgun until the police arrived.

Le Moyne endured his first controversial cremation, and soon others were asking to be cremated in the furnace or have a loved one incinerated there. Within two years, sixty applications were pending. Le Moyne declined all but a few: "An occasional cremation only will be permitted for the purpose of keeping the subject before the public eye," he wrote in 1878 after cremating a second body, a woman from Cincinnati.

Le Moyne's final message to the world about the wisdom of cremation and the folly of burial came in a treatise titled, "An Argument to Prove That Cremation is Preferable to Inhumation of Dead Bodies," which he dictated in one day at the age of eighty-two, "under the embarrassments of the infirmities of age, and under the depressing influences of a fatal disease." Le Moyne's parting words offer a comprehensive and eloquent argument for cremation and against burial. He was a socialist who'd found his cause and was taking it with him to the grave (in his case, of course, the furnace). Burial was very bad indeed in any way you might imagine, and here was his parting shot and a plea for the living to see the sense and humanity of fire.

Le Moyne minced no words and opened with a hit, oddly enough, on how burial prevented scavengers from doing their job, thus putting the living at risk from the poisons of decomposition. A body in the ground was protected from flesh-eating critters who were supposed to devour it, as laid out in the scheme of things:

Its [burial] practice endeavors to defeat the benevolent object of the Creator by hiding the body beneath several feet of imposed earth, thus rendering it inaccessible to the natural scavengers. Here it remains a mass of putridity for

*a period of ten or fifteen years, a prolific source of poiso-
nous emanations injurious to the living. The impression
has commonly prevailed that worms do their natural
work in the grave. This is an error. There can be no worms
where there are no larvae, and where there is no access to
the fly which deposits the larvae-producing egg. All
human experience proves the truth of this allegation, that
when disinterments are attempted, there is found, after
ten or fifteen years' deposit, only a mass of offensive, dis-
gusting, decomposing matter, without the presence of
worms.*

Worms or no worms, rotting human blobs in the earth were
not good.

Burial, argued Le Moyne, also exposed the hypocrisy of
Christians spending money on funeral and burial rather than
charitable pursuits:

*. . . when we devote portions, and often large portions, of
these accumulations to provision for expensive funerals
or costly monuments, we directly transgress the rule by
which our stewardship is to be guided. While great masses of the earth's population are living in heathenish dark-
ness, how dare Christian men devote so much of their
income to the gratification of their own pride and vanity
in aiding and abetting this sinful custom?*

To Le Moyne, cremation was the Great Equalizer:
"Cremation treats the body of a prince as it does that of the
peasant; the body of the king as that of the commoner; the
patrician as the plebian; the President of the United States as
the obscurest citizen. . . . The calcined bones of the poor are
precisely similar in form and beauty to those of the kings of the
world."

Cremation might also make the poor feel less hostility

toward the rich. Even in death, the rich strutted their position and prestige with self-important funeral processions and million-dollar mausoleums. The poor often wound up in a potter's field under a wood marker, if any marker at all, or tucked in a corner of a forgotten graveyard. What else but contempt would they have for the rich when they saw that even in death they were dwarfed and insignificant? "The innate hostility of men," wrote Le Moyne, "is provoked and cultivated by the mode of disposing of the dead bodies of the two classes which are oftenest at enmity with each other . . ."

Le Moyne reiterated the public health argument central to the cremationist movement: "Germs of disease cannot pass through the red hot flues, which connect the crematory retort with the chimneys, and retain their vitality, and the gases and vapors which escape into the atmosphere are deprived of vital germs."

Le Moyne was cremated and by the time his furnace shut down for good, around 1900, there'd been about thirty cremations there. By this time, fourteen states and the District of Columbia had crematories—New York with five, Pennsylvania four, California three. The country had cremated 15,963 of its dead by 1901, 5,000 alone that year. In Seattle, a man called Jacob Bleitz had designed the country's first "evaporator" cremation unit. By 1913 there were thirty crematories across the country, and the Cremation Association of America (today's CANA) was established by a doctor in Detroit troubled by bloated burial grounds there.

Two of the earliest cremation companies, both started in 1884, are still around today: Fresh Pond Crematory in Queens, New York, and the Cincinnati Cremation Company in Cincinnati, Ohio.

Fresh Pond was formed by the United States Cremation Company, which also set up an office in Manhattan to spread the word and enroll members. In the early days of cremation, most people choosing it were wealthy, educated, eccentric, or perhaps a mix of the three. They paid a premium to be incinerated in one of the brick-lined furnaces with the bronze doors in Fresh Pond's Hall of Incineration, as it was called, and for their cremains to be poured in a bronze urn and stored in a niche in the marble walls of the Fresh Pond Columbarium or on ornate shelves in the "Gothic Gallery." Some commissioned artists to sculpt busts of loved ones and placed them in the niche next to the urn. While a friend would be at the cemetery dropping flowers at a grave, they'd be opening the niche and depositing flowers there. Fresh Pond promoted cremation's romantic appeal. What better send-off into the Great Unknown than in "a robe of fire," as someone put it in an early ode to cremation, published in a 1922 Fresh Pond booklet:

Then wrap about my frame a robe of fire
And let it rise as incense, censor flung,
Until in ether pure, it may inspire
To greet the stars along the azure flung.

Fresh Pond drew famous clients—J. P. Morgan, Lou Gehrig among them—and solicited endorsements from doctors, professors, bishops, priests, ministers, and at least one steward of America's great capitalist machine, Andrew Carnegie.

Carnegie's cremation plug lacked the pizzazz of the romantics, but his point was unambiguous:

Cremation must be ranked as one of the greatest hygienic
improvements of a progressive age. Its universal adoption
is most desirable, and it is to be hoped that the people of
this country—always quick to be educated in matters of
reform—will soon recognize that cremation is something
with which religious prejudice or false sentiment should
not be allowed to interfere any more than with the sani-
tary expedients of modern life.

Sharing this page with Carnegie was, among others, Dr. W. F. McNutt, a professor of medicine at the University of California. McNutt reminded those who frowned on cremation that burial was no bed of roses while burning was a "purification":

> Most of the objections urged against cremation are the offspring of sentiment, superstition and usage. It is called unchristian, revolting to our senses, etc. To those who call incineration revolting, could they once witness the exhumation of a body that has been buried a year or two, they would never be buried themselves, nor advise their friends to be buried. In modern cremation there is nothing repulsive. It is a last baptism by incandescent heat; a purification by fire whereby the corrupt takes on incorruption, as the mortal takes on immortality.

For about seventy-five years Fresh Pond was the primary crematory in metropolitan New York. Cremations increased every year and peaked at 3,000 in the 1960s when other crematories opened and the number dwindled to its current 1,600-a-year rate. In Fresh Pond's 13,000 niches today are the cremains of some 50,000 people.

THE MEMORIALITES

By 1939 the national cremation rate had grown to 2 or 3 percent. The funeral and cemetery industries still had the death dollar locked in. Most people considered cremation antireligion, un-American, or they'd simply never heard of it except for perhaps a reference to widow-burning in India. It would be twenty-four years before the Catholic Church lifted its ban.

But 1939 turned out to be a pivotal year for cremation. That year the Reverend Fred Shorter formed People's Memorial Association in Seattle—the first death cooperative providing cremation exclusively for its members. The Great Depression had stirred farmers and sharecroppers to set up death cooperatives; everyone banded together to conduct their own funerals and bury their own dead. A funeral cooperative set up in 1929 in New Ulm, Minnesota, operates today as Minnesota Valley Funeral Home. These depression-era cooperatives had been strictly for burial.

The Rev. Shorter broke with this tradition. He was seen as a radical thinker and was thrown out of his church for far left political views. He wasted no time forming his own Church of the People, dedicated to spreading the "Ministry of the Socialistic Gospel," in the words of his friend, eighty-four-year-old Chet Kingsbury: "He just felt somewhere down the line that the working stiff wasn't getting a fair shake," Kingsbury told me, "He was for the humble working man; for the labor unions."

Shorter's Sunday services doubled as platforms for issues of the day and drew the likes of socialist presidential candidate Norman Thomas, southern sharecropper groups and other left wingers. Shorter decided that one of the services he would offer members was cheap and simple cremation through what he called a "memorial society."

"We weren't saying, these guys, the funeral directors, are robbing you," remembers Kingsbury. "Yeah, they were expensive. But our group was positive. We never said funeral directors were wrong, we just offered this. Fred would say: 'We take care of the disposal of the dead in a quick, economical and clean way.' That's all it really was." An early People's brochure echoes Kingsbury's memory: "Our aim is to make the services for the dead more meaningful and more beautiful than they are at present, at a fraction of the cost."

Membership in People's cost a dollar and provided you and your family with fifty-dollar cremations at Seattle's Bleitz Mortuary, named for its founder, the inventor of the evaporator cremator. Within a few years Shorter's idea caught on, and memorialites, as you might call them, started banding together throughout the country. By 1946 the first memorial society in the East—the Community Church Funeral Society—had formed in New York City. Today half a million people, most of them elderly, belong to 140 memorial and funeral societies across the country with more than 80 percent choosing cremation.

THE TWO TOMS

In 1971 a new kind of death society opened in San Diego, California—the Telophase Cremation Society. It began as a nonprofit memorial society, just like the Reverend Shorter's, but it soon evolved into a money-making enterprise that brought about the rise of a subdeath industry providing "direct cremation" and the scattering of cremains.

Telophase was the brainchild of Tom Sherrard, a patent attorney inspired by a law review article arguing that a mortician was not needed to dispose of a body, and Tom Weber, a biochemist/business man. Sherrard had been down on morticians for some time. He had joined the San Diego Memorial Society in 1958, the year it was founded, registering as the eighth person to enroll. By the late 1960s, Sherrard had become disenchanted with the funeral home serving his memorial society. The morticians were persuading fellow memorialites to buy merchandise they didn't want or need. The whole idea of the memorial society—providing inexpensive, simple cremation or burial—was being undermined by these profit-hungry opportunists. Sherrard read the law review article around 1970 and a spark went off: The memorialites didn't have to deal with these people, the morticians; they could be legally bypassed. All that was needed was someone to transport the dead person from the hospital morgue, nursing home, or wherever the person died, to the crematory and return cremated remains to survivors. Sherrard would need a partner to start his new cremation-only, morticianless memorial society, and he found one at the Medical Patents company, where he was on retainer. His partner would be the company president, a bio-chemist named Tom Weber.

"I asked him if he wanted to start a new non-profit group that would handle simple cremations," Sherrard told me. "I said to Weber, 'Let's have a direct cremation society.'" Sherrard brought Weber to a San Diego Memorial Society meeting in February 1971, and shortly thereafter the two Toms agreed on what would be a historic joint venture in the annals of the American death industry. Weber came up with the name—Telophase fittingly means the last stage of cell division—and America had its first cremation society.

Telophase's service was simple. People paid a $10 member-ship fee, just as they did to any memorial society, and when they died they were cremated. The cremains were scattered or put in an urn or box and returned to survivors. The price was $255, what most people got as a Social Security death benefit. Some people had their checks signed over to Telophase. You can imagine the reaction of local funeral directors, to whom people commonly paid $800 or $900 for just the casket.

In the early days, the two Toms did every thing themselves. They pulled up to the hospital morgue in a station wagon, picked up the body and drove it to a refrigerated holding morgue they set up in a southwest San Diego neighborhood. Someone who remembers this place is Ellsworth Purdy, a retired mortician in Portland, Oregon, who met Weber at a funeral directors convention in San Diego in the early 1970s. Purdy would go on to open a chain of twenty-one mortuaries and crematories in Oregon and Washington state before selling them to Service Corporation International in 1995. Purdy saw that cremation was starting to increase rapidly on the West Coast and wanted to see for himself what Telophase, which had received quite a bit of press, was up to.

During Purdy's visit, Weber took him to the Telophase "col-lection depot," as Purdy calls it. "The bodies were wrapped like mummies in an opaque plastic, with the name of the deceased written on the heads," remembers Purdy. "I was horrified! They were stacked on what looked like bakery racks, two feet by four. Maybe ten, fifteen bodies. That's how the bodies were stored, until the van came to take them to the crematory. He [Weber] was excited about this; he's a scientist, you know. He was looking at it from a purely practical point of view. I was horrified, I was taken aback. But I wanted to be a gracious guest; I didn't say anything."

This episode moved Purdy to commission a manufacturer to come up with what Purdy calls a "dignified" cremation container, in what seems like the spirit of the casketeers trying to stop the widespread use of cardboard boxes.

The two Toms delivered bodies from their morgue to a crematory. In the beginning, they were forced to go to Los Angeles because, as Sherrard tells it, local morticians had blocked them out of a crematory in National City, a San Diego neighborhood near the Mexican border, by telling the crematory owner that if he accepted a Telophase body he'd be boycotted by every funeral director in town. Telophase had signed a contract with this crematory and went to court to have it enforced. A judge eventually ruled in favor of Telophase.

After the cremation, Telophase usually gave the cremains to a Navy chaplain who scattered them at sea. California had strict rules on who could dispose of cremains: a minister or "registered cemetery agent," which meant someone working at a cemetery. Today, anyone can get a scatterer's license from California's state Department of Consumer Affairs, but cremains are supposed to be scattered only in a cemetery or at sea, at least three miles offshore. Some Telophasers opted to have loved ones' cremains scattered over a rose bush, as one of Weber's early customers did, or other spots chosen for personal reasons. When the scattering was done, Telophase sometimes conducted "memorial" services in San Diego's Balboa Park, people's backyards, or wherever survivors wanted to pay last respects.

Telophase formed as a nonprofit entity, but about a year later it was converted into a for-profit company. But it did not drop the "society" from its name and continued charging the membership fee. The difference between Telophase, which called itself a "cremation society," and the "memorial societies" confused people because a designation of "Society" is normally reserved for nonprofit organizations. This confusion remains today, as the number of the for-profit "cremation societies" has grown to hundreds and memorial societies number 140. People call memorial societies thinking they are cremation societies or not realizing there's a difference.

By keeping "society" in its name, Telophase set the standard for a horde of cremation businesses that followed. Most of them charge a membership fee and call themselves "societies," although in New York State for-profit businesses can't identify themselves as societies; you'll see plenty of Joe Blow Cremation Services, Jane Doe Cremations, but no John Smith Cremation Society. Recently, some have gotten the message and bypassed "society" for "alternative," like cremation specialist, Oregon Funeral Alternative.

Sherrard says he objected to Telophase becoming a for-profit entity but admits, with regret, he capitulated and stayed with the company for ten years. Although the two Toms accomplished their goal of letting people bypass the mortician and save lots of money, Sherrard believes the profit motive corrupted the idea. By 1981, Sherrard says he was being forced out of the company. He accepted a $70,000 buyout and hasn't talked to Weber since. Today he's working on a nonprofit group called "Unbroken Connections," which will log the biographies of cremated people in family archives.

In two conversations with Weber, held months before I talked to Sherrard, he never mentioned his old partner. Weber told me he started Telophase for two reasons: Memories of the indignities he suffered after being unable to find a funeral home in Oklahoma City to cremate his father; and his company was moving to New York, and he wanted to stay in San Diego.

"It was a horrendous, tremendous shock," Weber told me in a telephone interview, speaking of his father's cremation. "It took me several days and a lot of hassles and we had to have the body shipped to Tulsa for the cremation." When Medical Patents moved to New York, it was all Weber needed to pursue an ambition he'd been mulling over since the episode with his father: starting a company providing inexpensive cremations. Sherrard says he came to Weber with the idea, and Weber concedes Telophase was created after Sherrard brought him to the San Diego Memorial Society meeting in February 1971. Weber quit Medical Patents, giving up his $55,000 salary and company Cadillac, and Telophase opened an office in downtown San Diego.

Telophase had challenged the funeral industry's raison d'e-tre. An unorthodox service for the dead, concocted by a couple of San Diego professionals fed up with morticians, became a crusade. Weber was called on to speak at hospitals and universities on the benefits of cremation. He kept the message simple: Cremation was more dignified than burial. Cremation was more sanitary than burial. You didn't need a mortician. You didn't need to spend thousands on funeral and burial. The press covered Telophase with human interest articles: ". . . We honor the memory of the dead person and not the cadaver," Weber told a San Diego paper in 1973.

Telophase raised some of the same questions pioneering cremationists had raised ninety years before: Why drain a dead body and pump it full of embalming fluid to pretty it up for a few hours before lowering it into the ground forever? Why spend hundreds if not thousands of dollars on a fancy box called a casket? Why put the casket in a fancy holding tank called a burial vault? How the heck do you "protect" a corpse, and even if you could why would you want to? Why dress the dead in gowns and suits (and new shoes, for that matter?) The country wasn't burying pharaohs. The purpose of the cemetery was also questioned. Why, it was asked, should a chunk of land be wasted on a rotting corpse?

The morticians didn't take this assault lying down. The California funeral industry was determined to put Telophase out of business. The regulatory board and state funeral association charged Telophase with performing mortuary services without a license and eventually won on this front: California crematories must have at least one licensed mortician working there at all times. Telophase was also hit by two or three dozen individual lawsuits by individual mortuaries and cemeteries perturbed by this extreme variation of the way things had always been done.

Telophase persevered through the legal morass, with Sherrard as counsel. By 1977 it had conducted 3,000 cremations and listed 22,000 members. It eventually opened five other locations in Southern California.

COLONEL CINDERS

Telophase had started something big. In 1973 a cremation society modeled after Telophase, the Neptune Society, opened in San Francisco. Neptune's specialty was scattering celebrations. The founder was an eccentric retired chiropractor named Charles Denning who wore a goatee beard, a-la Colonel Sanders of Kentucky Fried Chicken, and told the media to call him Colonel Cinders, as he championed the savings and benefits of cremation and scattering and mocked morticians for bamboozling the public with useless merchandise for corpses. Colonel Cinders popularized scattering parties on chartered yachts. Newspaper articles from the mid-1970s show photos of Denning on his scattering yacht, reading a verse from the Bible as his wife stands by about to scatter a box of cremains. Like Telophase, Colonel Cinders charged $255 (although his membership fee was $20). By late 1977, Denning had ten offices, including three in Florida. He eventually franchised the operation, and today there are four independent Neptune Society businesses with an estimated half million members (all paying a $20 or $30 membership fee) in California, New York, and Florida.

As weird as this California fad seemed to many, the bottom line was not weird at all: People saved a bundle. *Florida Magazine* ended a piece on Denning in October 1977 with the story of an elderly couple that joined Neptune and used the $5,000 it had stashed away for funeral and burial for a trip around the world: "A month later, Denning says, he received a picture postcard from the couple, sipping aperitifs at a Paris cafe and thanking their new-found benefactor."

In the twenty-five years since Telophase arrived, California's cremation rate has climbed to 43 percent. The two Toms both say they started Telophase with the intention of doing good for society, breaking the stranglehold they felt morticians had on the public; making money was not the motivation. Weber says he started it from an "altruistic motive." After all, he gave up a good salary and a Cadillac for a career of schlepping dead bodies around, commuting by Schwinn bicycle and a modest standard of living—especially modest after paying off legal bills from fighting morticians taking him to court. Sherrard reminds me that he handled legal chores until he left in 1981.

Whatever the motivation of the founders of America's modern cremation movement, the American way of death had been challenged and transformed forever.

I WANT TO BE
CREMATED

The killing of animals also provided fat which was smeared on the body to assist the combustion. Animal and human fat was also sometimes used to seal the lid of the urn containing cremated remains.

—James Stevens Curl's *A Celebration of Death*

He opens the brick-lined cremation chamber and there is a pile of bones—the bones of an eighty-one-year-old woman incinerated twenty-four hours ago. Her body had been burned for ninety minutes at 1,500 to 1,700 degrees in the basement of Woolworth Chapel at Woodlawn Cemetery in the Bronx, New York, a few hundred yards from the last northbound stop of the Number 4 subway line, a few miles from Yankee Stadium.

"The feet go in first, so the main burner comes down on the

main part of the chest cavity, that'll make a complete cremation," says the operator, Rudy Fighera, a beefy man of forty-seven with a black beard and mustache covering a round, smiling face. It is a weekday afternoon in August 1994, and I'm on assignment to profile one of New York's veteran cremation operators. Rudy is from Yonkers, New York, just over the Bronx line. He's been Woodlawn's one and only one-man cremation crew since the crematory was installed in 1977 under this chapel built with funds from the fortune of the department store magnate who made "Five & Dime" a household word. Rudy had joined Woodlawn fresh out of high school in the late 1960s, and by 1977 he'd made it to gardener. He applied for the cremation gig and got it. At last count he had cremated near-ly 11,000 bodies. In recent years he's been getting four or five bodies a day, five days a week. In 1977, Woodlawn cremated 5 percent of its dead; today it's more than 15 percent.

Wearing rubber gloves, sunglasses, and dust mask, Fighera maneuvers his bulky frame into the bowels of the chamber and rakes the bones—foot-long bones within a white mangled clump of vertebrae. He uses a long pole with a broom head at the end of it and looks like someone going for leaves under a gutter. The bones are swept into a metal bucket which sits under an opening at the front of the chamber. Commingled within this mesh of what once had been are nails and wood ash from a pine casket.

"When a pacemaker explodes, you hear a loud pop," Fighera tells me. It's actually the battery inside the pacemaker that explodes. "Or if people put a bottle or can inside the cas-ket, they can explode, too. I'll usually find the pacemaker by the chamber door. Luckily, I haven't been checking on a cre-mation when anything's exploded."

Fighera puts down the broom, picks up a hand-held brush, sweeps the remains of the cremains into the metal box, and dusts the edge of the chamber. He grabs a small black box from a hydraulic lift behind him, takes a coin from it, and tosses it into the bucket. Like all the to-be-cremated, this woman had been assigned a number that is etched on the coin so her cremains are not mistaken for someone else's.

Now it is time to grind up the bones, and Rudy moves through a narrow walkway past the exhaust system—a jumble of giant blue pipes and water-squirting scrubbers (to comply with air pollution regulations) looking like a ship's engine room. A blanket hanging from a door jamb separates his office from the hallway. It is an unremarkable room with a cement floor and white cardboard boxes on a metal shelf. On Rudy's desk is today's *New York Post* with a headline blaring the latest on the drama of a corrupt Harlem police precinct. On a table in one corner is the electronic cremains processor, a blender-like contraption with a large aluminum pot on a square metal base with knobs and switches. Rudy places an aluminum rack over the pot and positions a vacuum hose over it. He dumps the bucket on the rack, picks out the coin, flips it back in the black box, and flicks on a very loud vacuum. Now it is time to sift out the nails. He grabs a padlock-shaped magnet, drags it through the pile, and a dozen or so are drawn instantly to it.

Rudy dumps cleaned cremains in the pot, sets a timer for thirty seconds, and flicks a switch. The sound is like the frantic roar of a milkshake blender behind a restaurant counter. The bones are churned to a grainy powder peppered with white flecks. It is a darker shade of grayish sand, in spots nearly black. "Sometimes the families put something inside the casket. They'll put some kind of powder or perfume or something; anything can change the color," Rudy tells me. Gold and silver teeth fillings give cremains a green hue.

Rudy dumps the cremains into a plastic bag, twirls it, ties it with a garbage bag tie, puts the bag in the black box, seals the lid, grabs a white cardboard box from the rack, and puts the black box inside. With packing peanuts stuffed in for a snug fit, Rudy slaps on a label, and writes in a name and address. They will either be mailed to survivors or picked up by a funeral director.

"It's a clean set up," Rudy says, looking over a list of the day's cases. "It's sanitary-looking. It's clean, it's light, it's airy. I don't know, I guess to me that's what cremation is, something light."

In 1937 *Reader's Digest* published "Light, Like the Sun," an essay romanticizing cremation and extolling the horror and folly of burial. Thousands of letters of praise poured in. It became a staple of procremation literature and was reprinted twice by *Reader's Digest* in the next thirty-five years. Written by forty-one-year-old Frances Newton, it told of her rite of passage into the cremation camp while searching for a grave for her ailing father. Along the way she discovered what was clearly to her the vanity, waste, and horror of burial and the beauty and prudence of cremation.

Her transformation came while browsing for grave plots at the local cemetery: "It was a cold, wet mid-December day and, as we looked at plots, a feeling of utter horror swept through me," she wrote. "There, in that manufactured park with its ghoulish artificiality, with its interminable monuments to bad taste, wealth, and social position, we were planning to place the body of a beautiful and dignified old man who had lived generously and loved beauty." The person escorting Newton through the cemetery brought her to the crematory. The attendant there turned out to be a friendly old codger. Newton asked him bluntly, "Does it burn? Like a bonfire?" meaning, of course, the body. "Have you ever looked into the sun?" returned the attendant. "You know how bright and clear it is? That is what surrounds the body and consumes it. Light, like the sun."

It's not clear whether Newton had ever looked into the sun before, but a victorious chord had been struck: "Light, like the sun. A sense of triumph came over me," mused Newton. "Sunlight over Father working in his garden. Sunlight on his white head as he sat on the terrace reading. The warmth of sunlight bringing life to growing things, falling benignly on the aging. 'When his time comes,' I told my aching heart, 'I shall bring him here.'" She didn't have to wait long. Father died a week after Newton's near-religious experience at the crematory. On the drive to the crematory to deliver his body, she couldn't resist a parting shot at the miserable burial ground: ". . . we passed the cemetery with its soot-stained stones and snow, its uncovered ugly clay where the earth had been freshly broken, and I had a great singing thankfulness that we were not to lay him there." And so it was on to the crematory and the moment of truth. She watched the casket disappear into the cremation room and, somewhat anticlimactically, that was that. No going out in a "robe of fire," no "incandescent baptism," to use a few choice metaphors from early cremationists. "And so we left him," concluded Newton. "Not for me the agony of knowing his frail body lay in the cold earth. All I knew on the empty journey home was that around the gentle, kindly old man there was 'light, like the sun.'"

Cremation let Newton avoid the horrors she associated with the cemetery and perform a philanthropic act. With the money she saved, Newton had the university where father had been a professor set up a scholarship fund in his memory: "Sometime in the autumn," she waxed sentimental, "a student will be called into the provost's office. There he will be told his withdrawal is not necessary, that funds are available. Father's memorial does not lie in a mound of earth and a stone."

Here was a solid hit against the American institution of burial in a magazine read by millions. Cremationists could not have asked for a better voice than Newton. She had brought one of their most important messages to a mass audience: Burial betrayed the vanity of humankind and was a big waste of money that could be spent on a good cause; cremation was brilliant and ethereal; burial was ugly, gloomy, a horror.

From time to time throughout the twentieth century, someone famous plugged cremation. H. G. Wells wrote of the "quivering bright flames" in an account of the cremation of his wife in *The Book of Catherine Wells*:

> *The coffin was pushed slowly into the chamber and then, in a moment or two, a fringe of flame began to dance along its edges. It was indeed very beautiful. I wished she could have known of those quivering bright flames, so clear they were and so eager, yet kindly living things. It was good to think she had gone as a spirit should go.*

Most people don't stay around to watch the actual incineration of their loved ones. One of the better descriptions of a cremation—as seen through a crematory porthole—appeared in a 1993 *New Statesman & Society* article: "In such intense heat [1,930 degrees Fahrenheit], the coffin burns away in ten or fifteen minutes. What you see is a clearly defined skeleton, ribs crumbling away to look like twigs. It lies very still on a bed of ashes in a roaring orange heat. A piece of plastic from the coffin flaps slightly near the skull. Everything is flaking, disintegrating into soft dove-grey ash. After an hour and a quarter, the skeleton is reduced to bones, or bits of bones, no more than six inches long."

REASONS TO BE CREMATED

Light like the sun and quivering bright flames aren't on the mind of everyone choosing cremation. Some think of the environment: What our grossly overpopulated earth definitely does not need is another body in the ground. Cremation reduces you to granules of calcium. You've essentially been returned to dust, back in the eternal mesh of energy and matter.

Some think of cost. Direct cremations go for as low as $350 compared to the $5,100 average cost of funeral and merchandise, which doesn't include your grave, the digging of and filling in of your grave (a $200 to $600 job), a headstone or marker, and incidentals, like hiring a performer for a graveside service and tipping the clergy with an honorarium. Governments sometimes cremate the homeless whose burials would bust their social services budget.

Average Joes are opting for outrageous cremation dispersals, like the man whose cremains were blasted into the sky in a fireworks rocket; hunters instructing friends to load their cremains like so many pellets into shotgun shells and pump them out over a favorite hunting spot; or the gentle soul from Washington State instructing his wife to bury his cremains in a Roy Rogers lunch box.

There is the fear-of-burial factor, dramatized nicely by Newton. For many, the thought of being vaporized is apparently less traumatic than rotting in the ground, although, as we've heard in previous chapters, some morticians and casketeers will tell you that a body with a good embalming in a steel casket, itself sealed in a vault, will be preserved for years, and there are exhumations to prove it.

The convenience factor has greatly influenced America's cremation revolution. With families scattered across the country, rounding up everyone for the funeral can be a logistics nightmare. Of course, a million factors come into play, like how close and large the family is and how far everyone has to travel to make it back for the funeral. There's also plenty of hostile relations out there with no interest in paying last respects to say, a, crotchety old uncle who just died in Kalamazoo. We're not a nation of John Boy Waltons or Ward Cleavers anymore. Without more than a smattering of family, what's the use of having a wake and funeral? And for that matter, as sad as it sounds, people left with tending to the final arrangements of a lonely old soul may ask, why buy a grave when no one's going to visit it?

Some elderly folk living far away from their children think

of their children's convenience when planning end-of-life details. It is a last selfless act, a great final show of consideration. Many of Gary Dougherty's clients at Dove Crematory & Funeral Chapel in Orlando, Florida, are senior citizens from the North who want their remains laid to rest back home but who don't want survivors burdened with flying down for a funeral and the logistics of shipping the body home. "They don't want to go through the fuss of a funeral service and so they give instructions to their children to have them cremated and the remains to be put in an urn and sent North," Dougherty says.

McDermott-Crockett Mortuary in Santa Barbara, California, receives nearly 900 bodies a year; 72 percent are cremated. It contracts with the two area memorial societies and charges members $623 for direct cremation, a price others would find hard to beat. "It's cheaper and easier to cremate here and forward remains back to wherever," says McDermott-Crockett general manager Bruce Bennett. "California's a fast-paced state. People say, 'We don't have three days for a visitation and church services. We have things we have to do.' Cremation is expediting what nature is going to do any way: Ashes to ashes, dust to dust."

Some of the cremation-minded don't take kindly to religion and tradition dictating what's proper for their corpse. There's an element of pride here: It's their body, their death, their private belief concerning death and the afterlife (or lack thereof). They don't appreciate religious institutions or family tradition dictating postdeath ritual to them. It is the irreverence of the atheist and the agnostic, the idealism of the New Age spiritualist, the pondering of the academic examining their death as they might other intellectual pursuits.

An agnostic's procremation argument goes something like this: With the spirit and/or soul dissipated to another plane or reality, you might as well eliminate the body in a two-hour blast of fire rather than commit it to a chunk of land—for which there is a great demand in our population centers—where it will undergo the dreadful fate of decomposition. And there are certainly things to spend funeral and burial money on.

This point is made by forty-nine-year-old Scott Von Stein of Mill Valley, California, who threw an elaborate cremation/scattering party for his mother: "When you die," Von Stein says, "your soul, if there is such a thing, that flees the body and goes to heaven. It seems more dignified to be cremated than having worms gobbling up your body in this dampened box for eternity." The issue was forced for Von Stein in late 1994 when his eighty-four-year-old mother died from a painful bout of emphysema. "I watched her die," he said. "She went, and in a sense, I was happy to see her go. The blood had drained from her face and she just didn't look like herself, certainly not like I'd want to see her in a casket. When a person dies, the soul, or whatever, is gone—it's gone! And what you see is a shell. It's nothing to deify."

After Von Stein arranged for his mom's cremation, 100 friends and family gathered at his place for a catered party. A magician entertained. Toasts were made to the grand old lady and the party climaxed at San Francisco Bay where everyone took a pinch of her cremains and flickered them on to the glistening water as fifty balloons drifted into the sky. What better way to celebrate his mother's life, Von Stein explains, than with a celebration? A successful realtor and champion bridge player, she loved to throw parties herself and wasn't one for solemn dirgey funerals: "She didn't want a maudlin service, she didn't want her friends to mourn her loss." As I talked to Von Stein our conversation turned to his feelings about death and burial and religion in America: "I think a lot of people don't have time for the Church, the hocus-pocus of religion concerning funerals and burials. The same old stuff is not cutting it. People are questioning the burial process. Look at the time and expense. We spent three thousand dollars for the party, and it was a hell-of-a party. What's wrong with cremation? When you consider

India and China, half the world is doing it."

Von Stein's right about India, the land where the funeral pyre is still common and some communities still burn widows alive (if husbands suffered untimely deaths). But the Chinese are a different story. They have long buried their dead until recent years with mushrooming populations in the cities now forcing China to cremate nearly 40 percent of its dead.

Talk to memorialites from the nation's 140 memorial and funeral societies and you'll likely get plenty of gripes about, if not scathing indictments of, morticians. "They're always looking for ways to get people to bury a lot of money in the ground," says seventy-seven-year-old John Blake, executive director of the Funeral and Memorial Societies of America (FAMSA) for five years until he stepped down in June 1996. FAMSA is the umbrella group for all memorial societies. One of the reasons Blake stepped down was to concentrate his efforts on running the Memorial Society of Dorr County, Wisconsin, where he lives. Blake is one of many memorialites who got into the death cooperative business because of a bad experience with a funeral director. Blake's came in 1985 when he traveled to Bremerton, Washington, to arrange for the cremation of his ninety-year-old mother. A mortuary charged him $1,000 for the task, and Blake found out later, after going through his mother's papers, that she had belonged to People's Memorial Society in Seattle and had a $340 cremation coming her way. Blake remembers asking himself, "Mother, why didn't you tell me?" Perturbed by this egregious overpricing, Blake returned home to Wisconsin and joined the local memorial society. He had found his cause and in a few years moved on to the nearby national office in Egg Harbor, Wisconsin, where in 1991 he became executive director.

Blake follows a long line of pugnacious memorialites anxious to take on the good old boy morticians they say are lurking in every community. These funeral-and-burial bound old-school funeral directors are more interested in making a profit than helping people bury or cremate their dead, says Blake. If they don't sell merchandise, they don't make profits, like any business. When I asked Blake why people can't fend for themselves, like they do for a thousand different purchases, and shop around for the mortuary they want, he told me: "Sure, you have to battle with used car salesmen, your bank, your real estate agent. What concerns me is these people [morticians] are doing this, engaging in a business transaction, when people are not able to fight back. And on top of it, the funeral industry has done a very good job of trying to convince the public they are professionals. They're not professionals, they're tradesmen. These guys—now they're trying to get into grief counseling. This is all a p.r. stunt to stay in touch with people to get their business. This is almost criminal."

Blake's successor, Lisa Carlson, carries as much if not more ill-will toward the Everyman funeral director. There's a sense with the memorialite that something will be rotten in Denmark no matter what changes have been made to the death industry. The changes have been considerable. Cremation itself is transforming the way funeral directors do business, and the federal government now regulates them with the Funeral Rule, which has done its part to keep opportunistic morticians in check. There's more competition in the funeral industry than there has ever been. Cremation societies have cut into their business. In some areas cemeteries sell caskets. Hundreds of consumer advocacy newspaper articles are published each year, many listing the prices they'll find at the local mortuaries. Funeral homes must give out price lists and aren't supposed to tell people things like grandpa must be embalmed and buried in a casket. Many people are arranging and paying for funerals and burials and cremations before they die, as recommended by America's most powerful lobby, the American Association of Retired Persons (AARP), so survivors aren't saddled with making this transaction when grief and confusion reign. The consumer protection crusade of the past thirty years has done some good.

Yet there will always be abuses in the funeral industry, and Blake can tell you about one happening in his own back yard in Dorr County, Wisconsin. He says he can't get the three local funeral homes to come down in their cremation price for Blake's members. So, he says, the hell with 'em. "I got a funeral director 150 miles away in Milwaukee who comes and picks up our members, brings them back to his crematory, and returns the remains, for $580," Blake told me. "The local boys are charging $1,200 to $1,500." For the handful of his members who want to be buried, Blake calls another Milwaukee mortician who performs the service for $1,100, less than a third of what the local boys charge.

A ROTO ROOTER IN YA

Another feisty memorialite is seventy-six-year-old Laurence Matthews, an officer of the Funeral Association of Central Washington State. He has no illusions about what's in store for a body when it arrives at the embalming table: "The corpse is gutted with preservatives, and the heart and insides have gone down the sewer," he told me with a chuckle. "All they wanna do is put a Roto Rooter in ya and pump ya full of formaldehyde. That makes you look good for three or four days. And what they don't tell you is there's a very small fly that gets into the casket. It has a long-term meal there." Matthews refers to the Phorid fly, which detects rotting human flesh from miles away. Along with leakers—mausoleum slang for bodies dripping fluid out of caskets—the Phorid fly is the nemesis of many a mausoleum tender.

I interviewed seventy-six-year-old Helen Rader, a retired registrar of voters in Columbia, South Carolina, in February 1994 when this book was conceived. She was one of six locals who had recently formed the Memorial Society of the

Midlands. (Cremations in South Carolina went from 597 in 1982 to 2,139 in 1992.) "A lot of our people are very interested in cremation," she told me. "They are drawn to the memorial society because of its lower cost. Funerals have gotten so very expensive. All that money doesn't do much good for anybody. There's a better use for the thousands of dollars you'd spend on a casket and vault. I personally don't want to spend thousands of dollars on a casket and a vault and cosmetic extras a good many funeral directors will tuck in if you let them. I just think it's a waste of money. I'll leave it to my church (Unitarians), or my children."

There are mellower memorialites, like John Buchanan, eighty-one years old, of Ventura, California, a retired speech professor who once held John Blake's executive director position, as well as the presidency of the Los Angeles Funeral Society. He got into the society business in 1966 after Ruth Harmer, author of *The High Cost of Dying*, spoke at his college and mortuary students picketed her. When I spoke to Buchanan he didn't linger on the merchandising tricks of morticians but focused wistfully on the philosophical. He says people who join memorial societies "have joined a select group that looks at death as a part of life that has to be planned for." No final farewells to a lifeless body for Buchanan: "Once life is gone the body is corruptible. There's nothing there that's spirit. It's so many chemicals and matter. Maybe you have to mature to understand why someone chooses cremation. You have to see the flowers grow and die, the peaches dropping to the ground from the trees and others growing in their place. You've got to call it quits some time."

When I first talked to fifty-two-year-old Bill Goben in the spring of 1995, he was preparing to sail from Seattle to Mexico to pick up a twenty-one-ton rig and sail it back to Seattle. Goben owns and operates the Blue Dolphin Society, Seattle's cremains scattering company. Goben was going to pick up Blue

Dolphin's new vessel, from which cremains would be tossed overboard—usually over the Pacific Ocean, Puget Sound, Lake Washington, or off the San Juan Islands. Once in a while a Blue Dolphin customer requests airborne service, and Goben charters a twin engine plane; at 7,000 feet cremains are whooshed out of a tube over Mount Rainier, Mount Baker, the Olympic Mountains, or the Cascades.

Goben's scattering career began in 1975 when his best friend, a sailing comrade, died of cancer. "He wanted his ashes out there," Goben told me, meaning somewhere between Seattle and the Hawaiian islands, his friend's favorite sailing ground. How could Goben refuse? He set sail for Hawaii and about 1,000 miles out to sea performed his first "dissemination," as he calls it. People got wind of Goben's favor—this was during the time the two Toms and Colonel Cinders were popularizing scattering—and he was soon getting calls from senior citizens and their children requesting he scatter a loved ones cremains for them. Goben obliged, charging just $15 to cover the cost of permits and expenses. With Seattle being a cremation stronghold—Cremationist Rev. Shorter started the first cremation society there in 1939—demand grew. Goben said he decided to move from granting favors to starting a real business after hearing an elderly woman tell him she had to sell her house because she spent so much on her husband's funeral. Like the two Toms and the memorialites, he'd been inspired to give people an option over the traditional funeral director, and in 1981 he founded Blue Dolphin. It's a profit making enterprise, but Goben keeps his price down to a basic fee of $75. The price includes an exact scattering spotting by nautical measurement so survivors know precisely where grandpa was let go so they can join him when their time comes. Goben performs about 150 disseminations a year, including thirty or forty from the sky, for which there's an extra fee. Other extras include faraway dispersements, like off the Yucatan Peninsula—one of Goben's stops during runs to Mexico—and photographs or a video of the ceremony, provided by Blue Dolphin Productions.

SCATTERING EPIPHANIES

There's a romance to scattering on the water. Yes, we're talking five or seven pounds of crushed bone, but bones of someone you love, and they are blowing into a large beautiful body of water surrounded by islands, filled with fish and various sea creatures. Weather permitting, sunlight will glisten off the rippling water, a breeze will sweep across your face, sea birds will swoop above you. For many the experience subdues or at least postpones the pangs of sorrow and emptiness and the coming to terms with the end, both theirs and yours. The way Goben puts it is:

> *"It's not like going to a funeral. There's a corpse and a casket and it's lowered into the ground. I don't like the thought of rotting. The people I deal with are serious about what they're doing, but they seem to be at a lighter level. When they want to reminisce, they go to park and sit quietly. Or a marina, or maybe they have dinner at a restaurant on a pier, and they just sit and look out across the beautiful islands and think about their loved one."*

Goben has scattered the cremains of a few thousand individuals and recalls many epiphanies as nature seemed to acknowledge the sacredness of the occasion with a flicker of breeze or nuance of filtered sunlight. In the fall of 1995 he packed a family of ten—father, three children, grandchildren—on his motor boat for a dispersement of the man's wife on Puget Sound. It was a beautiful sunny day, no wind. They came to a lighthouse near Vashon Island with snow-capped Mount

Rainier in the distance. Here was the spot. Goben killed the engine and the boat floated gently as Goben fetched the container of cremains and the family gathered their roses:

"I put the ashes in the water—the ashes are really dusty, it's like a cloud of dust in the water. And everybody had thrown flowers in and said goodbye to grandma. Then all of a sudden a current turned us around, and we circled the ashes and the flowers, and the cloud of dust was sinking into the water, and right in the middle of this patch of flowers was the reflection of this big gorgeous white mountain with blue sky behind it. And just at this time a jetliner was taking off and it was silhouetted against the mountain. It was so beautiful. Everyone just stopped and stared."

Goben's emotional zenith probably came when he disseminated his father's cremains in 1988 from the family's sailboat. After dumping them overboard, Goben says he "walked over and untied that old lawn chair that Pa used to sit in for hours while he fished—he was a great fisherman. And I slipped it into the ocean behind him. Then his little grandson, Danny, asked his grandma, 'Do you think Grandpa will be able to find his chair, Grandma?'"

The romance of scattering can cross over into an environmental statement. "People are thinking and feeling that if they go into the ground, they decompose over fifty years or so, to, basically, skeletal remains," Goben says. "And then the bones hang around for a while. We're in an era of recycling. People look at cremation like that: 'Hey, my calcium goes right back, and it'll be used by all the sea critters out there.' Cremation is not a detriment to the environment. The oyster fishermen grind up their shells and put them back in the ocean just like people's calcium in the form of dust is going into the ocean. I think people like that, getting back into the chain . . . People

The American grave vault, required at most cemeteries, evolved from the "mortsafe"—a cage-like contraption installed over graves to thwart body snatchers. The photo above shows an iron mortsafe at a grave in East Hauxwall, Yorkshire, England.

The Western Undertaker

Entered April 17, 1861, at South Bend, Ind., as Second-class Matter, Under Act of Congress, March 3, 1879.

Vol. XXXIII   OCTOBER, 1910   No. 10

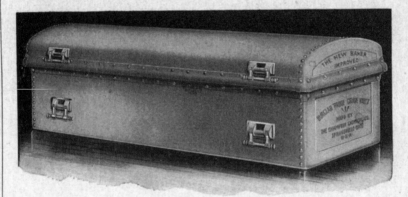
By the end of the 19th century, the metal grave vault was a fixture on America's burial scene. Making it on the cover of the October 1910 Western Undertaker *was the burglar-proof Baker vault.*

This burial vault at the cemetery in Hardin, Missouri, held its ground during a massive flood in the summer of 1993 that washed much of the burial ground away.

Americans have had
plenty of burial con-
tainers to choose from
since cabinetmakers
started banging them out
for the first settlers in
the 17th century. The
photo below shows a
heavy-duty metallic
unit, probably from the
late 19th century.

Napoleon's Tomb is an elegant
sarcophagus.

Bill Clendaniel, president of Mount Auburn Cemetery in Cambridge, Massachusetts, stands in the basement columbarium in the cemetery's Story Chapel. Elegant bronze urns occupy the "niche" compartments on the wall.

One of the country's first and most beautiful crematory-columbaria is Fresh Pond in Queens, New York.

Jeri Lyons, one of the founders of the Rootin Tuttin Toten Tutors, in Nashville at the 1996 conference of the memorialites.

Speakers at the National Funeral Directors Association's convention in recent years have included *Ed Bradley* (above), *of* 60 Minutes *fame, and husband and wife political consultants, James Carville and Mary Matalin* (below).

Rudy Fighera performs another cremation, at Woodlawn Cemetery in the Bronx, New York, The final stage is grinding the bones to a grainy powder in an "electronic cremains processor."

don't want to be pumped full of poison to decompose in fifty or 100 years when cremation does it with heat in twenty minutes. People would much rather have their elements in the food chain than making a big dead poison spot in the ground. That's what you've done when you get buried."

Like many cremationists, Goben reserves a barb or two for funeral and burial. He has a kind of insouciant disdain for what he sees as a barbaric, wasteful, unsanitary practice. But he doesn't carry the defiant tone of a John Blake, or the condescending air of some cremation advocates who would have you believe all funeral directors are crooks out to exploit your grief. Goben chuckles when telling the story of friends who inherited grave plots, sold them, and used the money to vacation in Las Vegas.

One of Goben's clients was sixty-six-year-old Lorene Herr. Her husband, Ben, a navy veteran, specified in his will that he wanted to be cremated and scattered on the water. When he died, Lorene called navy officials and they told her they'd scatter him but no one was allowed on board. Sorry, military protocol. Herr asked a local mortician if there was an alternative; he sent her to Blue Dolphin and Goben obliged.

It was to be a fairly large scattering party—Herr, her three children and their spouses, an adopted son, a few grandchildren. Goben rented a yacht, and on 8 October 1994, they shoved off the peninsula city of Anacortes, north of Seattle, toward the San Juan Islands. Herr related her scattering story to me on the phone in February 1996. She said she was still dealing with the loss of her husband and was grateful to Goben for taking her calls when she needed to talk to someone. She had been interviewed for a Blue Dolphin promotional video and had nothing but lavish praise for Goben: "He's a very, very, good, kind person."

Herr remembers,

"We had a beautiful, beautiful yacht, and the captain and

Bill [Goben] were so kind and good to the family. Bill scattered and read the obituary. He scattered them from an urn and at the end he just tipped it over and the ashes were all gone. We were in a stationary spot; they have the longitude and latitude of where it went. I have it arranged so I can be scattered in the exact same spot. We had flowers and bouquets for all the children, and we dropped them into the water. This to me was a very moving ceremony. It was very sad, but it was a good goodbye. We were able to say our goodbyes. He was a retired naval man, he had it all written down; we all knew that's what he wanted. No funeral service. I did what he wanted, it was the last thing I could do for him. It was extremely beautiful. Very peaceful. The water was nice. No wind, lots of sunshine, and the San Juan Islands are beautiful. But you can't help but be sad; it can be very sad. It's still hard being alone without my husband, trying to keep things going and moving along as he would want. You have to keep your head up and keep on moving if you want to stay alive. There are many stages of this grieving that's hard to get at."

After the scattering Herr held what she calls a "remembrance get-together" at her home: "So many, many people came by the house; it was such a comfort to have these people come by the house. We called it remembrance day."

OFFSPRING OF COLONEL CINDERS

The "you-don't-need-a-mortician mantra" is hammered home by cremation societies across the country. "Thank you for your interest in cremation," reads the opening of the World Wide Web site of The Cremation Society of Idaho. "More families every day are choosing cremation because, it is simpler, more economical and more dignified than the traditional funeral. We feel that the most caring thing you can do for your family is to prepare in advance. Preplanning eliminates any confusion about your wishes. All records are held in strict confidence. The Cremation Society of Idaho is fully licensed by the Idaho State Board of Funeral Service. There is not a need to use a funeral home. One call to us when you need us, is all that is necessary! Our charges for a simple cremation, at the time of need is $895. If you will take the time to register with us [a $30 fee] the cost is $770."

A thorough hit on the traditional American funeral and burial comes in the brochure of the Neptune Society of Northern California, offspring of scattering guru Colonel Cinders. In Neptune of Northern California's, "Considerate Decision" brochure, company president Tom Simonson writes:

"It is not uncommon for final [funeral and burial] expenses to exceed $10,000, given the cost of caskets, burial vaults, embalming, and other funeral and cemetery goods and services. We ask: Is this really necessary? What good does a big funeral do? It can do nothing for the person whose life has ended. For those who grieve, a sincere but simple memorial service can do as much to lighten their sorrow and honor the life of the one they loved. It is the spirit and the memory that lives on—the rest is vanity."

Neptune's fancy brochure looks like a menu a waiter in a tuxedo would hand you. The cover illustration shows a seagull in blue-white sky. A palate of choices are offered on cream-colored pages with blue headings. Sharp color photos show a scattering yacht near the Golden Gate Bridge and the lavender domed San Francisco Columbarium. There seems to be a cremation package for everyone on this palate, from a no-nonsense direct cremation, with cremains packed into a cardboard box for pickup at the crematory for $895 to a "basic cremation service with sea scattering private service," on board Neptune's yacht, the *Naiad*, for $1,590. If you're not the scattering type, there's plenty of "interment" options: Cremation with simple garden interment; memorial garden interment, columbarium garden interment, columbarium niche interment. Also offered are precremation funeral services—the all-important first step to selling cremation merchandise, as casketeers will tell you— and bodiless memorial services at the Neptune Chapel. There's no extra charge for "insertion witnessing," the cremation equivalent of watching the casket lowered into the grave, practiced in Hindu and Buddhist cremation rites. Add $30 to your bill for Neptune's membership fee; $9 for death certificate; $7 for a "permit of disposition"—a record of what you authorized Neptune to do with your body and cremains, required by the state of California—and you have a final price-of-death tally.

Neptune of Northern California owns the original Telophase Society of the two Toms fame. There are now six offices in Southern California. Mary Lou Stebbins manages Telophase's Orange County office. She got into the cremation business in 1987, in her fiftys, after a career as an office manager in an unrelated field. "The majority of our families are middle class," she says. "A traditional funeral is highly emotional, and a lot of people are just reluctant to have one. They say they just want simplicity. They just want a simple cremation." Stebbins will cremate you and have your cremains ready for pickup in a cardboard box for $741.94. Price includes the corrugated cardboard box you're to be cremated in. Her membership fee is $20. For an extra $75 you can have cremains shipped to survivors or scattered at sea by a Telophase scatterer. (Sorry, no survivors allowed on board.) If you want to be there for the dissemination, you'll have to charter Telophase's *America II* yacht for $595, with room for forty-five, shoving off near San Diego's Ocean Beach. Or you can take your own boat;

make sure you're at least three miles out before scattering. Also make sure you register with the Environmental Protection Agency's "Ocean Dumping Coordinator," a requirement of the federal government.

I CAN'T SCATTER

Christine Purificato, 48 years old, operates the Cincinnati Cremation Company with her her husband. It was one of the country's first cremation businesses, founded in 1884, the same year as Fresh Pond Crematory in Queens, New York. The Purificatos live at a house at the crematory. They've been cremating about seventy people a month since they took the job in 1985 after Christine's husband lost his job with the Army Corps of Engineers. He responded to an ad in the paper for a crematory operator, and they've been there since.

"I never thought about death, about what I was going to do with me, until I came here," Christine says. "If you want to know the truth, I would choose cremation now. You have to do something with yourself, and cremation is quicker than burial and less expensive. Whether you go in the earth or the cremation chamber—it's cleaner, it's neater, it's faster. I don't know. Some people don't want dirt on them; my mother doesn't want to be in the ground with bugs."

Purificato says all this discussion of what to do with one's dead body leaves her a bit tongue-tied, despite eleven years at the crematory. She does get sad when people don't bother to pick up the cremains of someone they are legally responsible for—it's not always family or relatives—or they tell her to put them in any old place in the columbarium. I've heard this from several morticians over the years—people simply abandon cremains at the crematory or mortuary. "Some people just flat out don't care," says Purificato. "I know funeral directors with boxes and boxes [of cremains] in their basements. People just don't want them. You'll get a husband and he tells us to stick her [cremains] any place. This is his wife he's talking about; that's sad. They let us pick a spot [in the columbarium] and just mail us a check and go their merry way."

Purificato gets some unusual requests, like the family that wanted someone's cremains divvied up into fourteen containers: "The family wanted bits of him scattered in different areas of the world where he'd been." When it comes to scattering, count Purificato out. "I can't scatter, I just can't give him a fling, just throw him away," she says, referring to her father, one of her customers. "It's just like throwing someone away. I don't know, I feel funny about it. When you're dead the soul is gone, but it is a shell left behind and you can't just throw it away. To me, it's still my father; it's my father, his shell. He walked around in it his whole life, even though now it's been reduced to bones; it was still him. Just like when your skeleton is in the cremation chamber, it's still you. My sister wants to put her ashes in a balloon and just let it go. She says this way she wouldn't be takin' up no space. She's just a practical girl, I guess."

Cemeterians will tell you the pitfalls of scattering. Bill Tate, superintendent of Laurel Hill Cemetery in Saco, Maine, sells full-sized granite headstones for cremation graves. He tells clients about to scatter in the nearby Atlantic Ocean or Saco River to think again: "Don't cast away the cremated remains," he tells them. "Don't cast them away. Put them aside for a moment and think about what you're going to do. We've had a few survivors who scattered come back to buy a spot to put the name on. They know something is missing when they don't memorialize a person."

Simplifying the question—to cremate or not to cremate— is author Robert Fulghum, a retired Unitarian minister from Seattle. "No matter what you do, sooner or later, you're dust," he told me shortly after the release of his 1995 book, *From*

Beginning to End—The Rituals of Our Lives. "In the larger view of things, sooner or later the earth will fall into the sun and we'll be cremated that way." I called Fulghum because one of the chapters of his book was titled, "A Cemetery View." It shows a photo of Fulghum sitting on a chair on top of his pre-paid grave. He is a sailor and wanted his cremains scattered at sea, but his children wanted them buried so they would have a grave to visit. So he shopped for a grave plot and wrote about his ritual of sitting on his grave to contemplate his "finitude."

Jack Springer reminds me that statistics show the older a person gets the more likely they are to choose cremation: Their body has withered away; in effect it has betrayed us and is no longer the trusty partner it once was.

"When a person has reached their 80s and 90s, their bodies have failed them," Springer says, "They remember the young body. I'm sixty-five and I consider myself in my mid-thirties. The stats say I have twenty-two years to go. I will have no great feel for a body that's worn. This romance with the body—if you have a teenage son you lost, you want to remember him as that teenage son. But you can't make that eighty-five-year-old look like a good eighty-five-year-old. The old shell is gone, and the young spirit is not encumbered."

AMERICAN

WHIPPING BOYS

Until recently, little has been said about the most irrational and weirdest of the lot, lying in ambush for all of us at the end of the road—the modern American funeral.

—from *The American Way of Death*

American funeral directors have been taking it on the chin for years. The idea of turning a profit off the dead does not sit well with a lot of people, no matter how good the intentions of the mortician. And it hasn't set well for a lot of people since the colonists arrived in the seventeenth-century. Massachusetts, for one, passed laws as early as the mid-seventeenth century forbidding extravagant funerals and processions. With all the needs of the living, how could people of faith with good conscience spend precious currency on mourning gloves and other lavish trappings for these celebrations of the dead?

But the dead still needed to be prepared, containerized, and buried, and someone would rise to the call.

With the growth of cities after independence from English rule, came an increase in population and the resulting increase in the number of dead and a corresponding demand for coffins and livery service for funeral processions. Cabinetmakers so inclined seized the moment and began specializing in coffins and delivery of the dead to the graveyard and America's "Dismal Trade," as the business of undertaking had been called in England, was born. Dismal though it may have been, it was a trade nonetheless, and the cabinetmaker was in it to turn a profit, just as the druggist, grocer, banker, or anyone else depending on their livelihood to earn a living.

By the Civil War some undertakers moved beyond the role of coffin maker–body transporter: They brought the funeral to the home, lugging the coffin into the parlor where the body was prepared and laid out for final viewing. Now families could be relieved of the custom (and burden) of tending to their own dead. By the 1870s embalming was coming into its own and the first undertakers' trade journals appeared. By the 1880s the first funeral parlors appeared: No longer did the home have to be way station of the dead; survivors could now bring the body of their beloved to the funeral parlor where they would be embalmed and laid out for a wake.

Gradually the undertaker assumed the role of guardian of the dead. They organized and formed associations. The first came in 1864—the Undertakers' Mutual Protective Association of Philadelphia. Sixteen years later, twenty-six Michigan embalmers got together and formed what eventually became NFDA, the funeral directors association detailed in Chapter one. About this time, maverick undertakers started calling themselves funeral directors and a debate arose over the role and status of the embalmer versus the fellow conducting the wake and running the business. By the turn of the century, an energetic industry of suppliers—casketeers, vault makers, hearse manufacturers, and embalming chemical companies—was evolving. By the 1920s, many people had stopped laying out their dead at home, except in rural areas, and the era of the modern funeral home was at hand.

A RESPECTABLE TRADE

Despite, or maybe because of the bum dismal trade rap, undertakers strove for respectability and association leaders rallied the troops at conventions. One was Charles A. Miller, an early NFDA treasurer. Miller reminded his audience at the 1903 convention that the industry brimmed over with fine individuals, including the casketeers and hearse makers scrambling to bring them the finest merchandise:

> *Don't you know, Mr. President, that nobody but ladies and gentlemen are engaged in this business any more, and it is being conducted in a professional manner, in a decent, respectable manner, and the finest talent in the land, the finest skilled mechanics that can be had, are employed in producing the goods that we are using, and don't you know he and every one is trying to outdo the other fellow, who makes coaches, freight wagons, funeral cars, etc., is determined the casket fellow shan't get ahead of him, and it is impossible to make anything but an elegant display of your funeral work.*

By 1909 Miller had made it to NFDA president. That year he reported to the faithful that things were looking rosy indeed, and people weren't picking on the undertaker the way they used to:

Look all over this broad land of ours and see the people begging the funeral director to become mayors and public officials. They are looking upon us now with more respect and confidence than any one else. (Applause) I recollect, Mr. President, twenty-three years ago how the newspapers would talk about us and our conventions. You would pick up the Cincinnati Enquirer and you would see, 'Stiff Hunters Assembling Here.' People looked with contempt upon us and said, 'What have you fellows got a meeting for?' Don't you know that every city in the United States is now begging for us to come to their city to hold our convention? They say, 'come and have dinner with us, stay all night with us, stay a week and come back next year again.' See how nice those people talk about us. So we go on progressing and progressing.

Miller's hyperbole was matched in transcendental spirit by undertaker B. F. Bracken, president of the Kansas Funeral Directors Association, who sprinkled his 1909 convention address with references to the "Chinese moralist Lao Tse" and Sir Isaac Newton. At times he sounded like he'd been reading Nietzsche—"True, night's noon has been passed, and standing tiptoe one can discern the first breaking of the day. Already the suffused light of the sun is kissing away night, and dispelling the morning mists from the barren ice-clad peaks of the eastern mountains. The shades and the gloom of ignorance and of prejudice are disappearing."

In a June 1909 address, Bracken bristled with the super-charged optimism of someone who'd been to the mountain top:

I hope the grouch is not present this morning. . . . I hail the man and the woman whose faces reflect the song in their life, and I want to strike hands with you in the determined purpose to make this convention a pleasant vacation, a trip to the mountains, a sojourn by the seashore, an airship ride through the clouds, a stroll through fragrance-laden gardens, a rest beneath the shade of the trees, a feast of good things, the peaches and cream of life.

Coming down to earth, Bracken told his audience to beware of the uncultured colleague, the clod who might wreck the reputation that progressive embalmers and undertakers were trying to cultivate. He singled out a Kansas undertaker who, "when sorrowing friends were grouped at the open sepulcher, turned to the pall bearers and in a stentorian voice said, 'Here, fellers, let's get this thing out of here,' having reference to transferring the casket from the hearse to the grave. This man is still a practitioner in Kansas, more fit to command a gang of white wings, charged with the gathering and disposition of the city garbage."

THE BIG HIT

The funeral industry grew through the first half of the twentieth century, enduring criticism from cremationists, discussed in Chapter three, and journalists and social critics questioning the practice of profiting off the dead. The nature of the work made them an easy target, as is the case today and probably will be indefinitely. Find someone who doesn't chuckle or raise an eyebrow when funerals, burial, cremation, and related topics pop up in conversation. Newspaper editors never fail to indulge in cutsey headlines for death industry stories: "Plan for Lake Crematory Fires up Nearby Residents," chortles a headline in the *Daily Commercial* of Leesburg, Florida (August 1993); "Ghoul Rules: Kronick Moskovitz Cleans Up with Class Action Undertakings and Moves to Bury the Competition," quips the *Daily Journal* of Los Angeles (February 1995) in a piece about huge settlements in California cremation scandal cases. Writers drawn to satire can't resist the irresistible target of the funeral director. In 1909 someone writing for the *Chicago News* enjoyed a few laughs over the advertising efforts of Baltimore morticians: ". . . the funeral directors of Baltimore seem anxious to convince citizens and strangers within the gates that, contrary to what naturally might be expected, they do not charge stiff rates. Emblazoned boldly on the dead walls is every sort of inducement to die and be laid away by one of these cheerful planters who will not profit by your having lived until after you quit living. Some of these propositions seem so immensely more economical than going on living, and are couched in such inviting terms, that one can hardly restrain one's self from taking advantage of them. The joy of having one of the boasted embalmers work on him must be very great, according to the advertisements. The process of being embalmed is made to sound as refreshing and desirable as an egg shampoo or a face massage. . . ." (Early twentieth-century cemetery entrepreneurs took a little egg on their face in *The Loved One*, a best-seller published in 1949—subsequently made into a movie—satirizing the American "memorial park" cemetery.)

Things didn't start to get rough for the funeral industry until the early 1960s. The stage had been set by magazine articles and books critical of the industry, including "Can You Afford to Die?" published in 1961 by the *Saturday Evening Post*. The big hit came in 1963 with publication of *The American Way of Death*. The author was the late Jessica Mitford, a British aristocrat-turned-communist-turned-social-crusader who died at age 78 in July 1996. Her husband, a union attorney, had set up a memorial society in Berkeley, California, in the 1950s and encouraged his wife to read the funeral industry trade journals if she wanted material for a book on the greatest of all capitalist exploiters. Mitford heeded his advise.

Her book condemned funeral directors as embalming fanatics and casket peddlers scheming to wrench money from the most vulnerable of prey—survivors mourning the death of a loved one. It got rave reviews and was an instant best-seller. It sold nearly a million copies and was translated into several languages, giving foreigners a particularly revolting American indulgence to marvel over. Critics gave rave reviews. *The New York Times Book Review* said the book was "about the high financial cost of dying in America and the immeasurably greater human cost of maintaining a way of death, which, in its unspeakable ugliness, its self-deception, sentimentality and perversion of the most fundamental attitudes toward existence, has never been approached by any other society, however technically 'backward.'" *The New Yorker* wrote: "A brilliant journalistic case against the whole funeral industry." And the *Saturday Review*: "One should certainly pass this book by if one's whole family is immortal. Otherwise it is the most exhaustive, documented explanation available of the ambush you and your family are inevitably walking into, unless you are lost at sea or vanish in an atomic war." (*The High Cost of Dying*, another book critical of the funeral industry published in 1963, was overshadowed by Mitford's work.)

With a severe and unforgiving attack, Mitford portrayed the "funeral men" as bumbling fools determined to be considered professionals even as they bamboozled the public with claims that embalming protected society from disease and caskets and vaults protected the dead from the elements and ground critters. "Gradually, almost imperceptibly, over the years the funeral men have constructed their own grotesque cloud-cuckoo-land where the trappings of the Gracious Living are transformed, as in a nightmare, into the trappings of Gracious Dying," explains Mitford in typically mocking fashion. Mitford had nothing good to say about the industry (she also trashed cemeteries and florists) until the end, when she noted that some mortuaries were providing inexpensive cremations and burials for memorial societies, like the one her husband operated.

Mitford's prose was crisp, her voice charged with condescending wit. At times she teetered into nasty insults, like when she accused the funeral men (few women worked in the field until the last twenty years or so) of being cry babies, convinced they were victims of a conspiracy when any criticism came their way: ". . . they snarl at the world from the pages of the funeral trade press, like angry dogs behind a fence unable to get [sic] to grips with the enemy."

Easy targets, the morticians and association officials Mitford interviewed. She grilled them over the rationale for embalming, protecting corpses, and charging what they did. Even a crafty politician would be hard pressed to finagle a convincing defense on these issues and the folks Mitford called on offered defensive, unconvincing, if not ludicrous, responses. Mitford spent a chapter tearing apart NFDA's party line that embalming was a sanitary practice protecting the public's health. She debunked the idea that a hermetically sealed casket would protect the corpse. She certainly wasn't buying arguments the funeral men articulated, like the benefits that embalming and gussying up the body provided—the "last memory picture," in the form of the person laid out at a wake, providing the closure we all need when confronted with the death of someone we love, an argument still made today by morticians, casketeers and grief counselors. It ain't over—our realization that someone we love is indeed gone forever—it is said, until we see their dead body. Only then can we get on with the business of closure and grief resolution, a buzz word today among therapists, counselors and nurses working in a subfuneral cottage industry tending to the bereaved.

Mitford wasn't buying the last memory picture. She also didn't go for the supply-and-demand defense the funeral directors gave her—that they were simply providing what people wanted, otherwise how could they still be in business?

The American Way of Death was absurd, wasteful, and perverse in many ways, but Mitford didn't talk to many morticians, or at least only wrote about those who came off as nincompoops or opportunists. She opted for the "broad brush" trashing style of gotcha journalism. There was another story here—one Mitford no doubt had no intention of, or, she might say, no reason for telling—and that was the story that some people wanted to see grandpa embalmed and laid out in a $3,000 casket. Some people not only had money to blow on postmortem excess (this was postwar boom time) but chose big gaudy funerals with big gaudy caskets as a show of status and their own idea of a respectful farewell. After friends and family paid last respects at the wake, the world outside would know someone important, someone well known and someone who was probably loved was on their way to the cemetery in a caravan of limos escorting the hearse through the streets of the community.

Humans have always made it a point to honor their dead with pomp and circumstance, at least those we love, those we were supposed to have loved, and the great and powerful. The Egyptians are the most familiar example, mummifying up their dead with elaborate embalming, drying and wrapping and entombing their pharaohs in the great pyramids with precious artwork of gold and all the amenities of life (sometimes including mummified bulls and other animals they'd be needing when they awoke from 3,000 years or so of the temporary sleep they were experiencing.) Like the Egyptians, many postwar Americans had the blood and water and innards removed from their bodies and refilled with embalming fluids. In the nineteenth century, some even went for the mummy cases discussed in Chapter two.

Some survivors wanted to see grandpa in suit and shiny shoes and grandma in chiffon gown and pink slippers, deposited in a big box, often made of bronze, copper, or stainless steel and lined with fluffy satin pillows and mattresses, one more time, or at least they thought they did. Or at least no one had a gun at their heads forcing them to engage in what Mitford would insist was a revoltingly exploitative act benefiting no one but the greedy mortician who orchestrated this shameless racket.

The problem that Mitford exposed was a structural one: Death had been allowed to be wildly commercialized in America since embalming took hold during the Civil War, and perhaps it should not have been. The only conclusion to be drawn from Mitford's book was that funeral directors had concocted a grand seduction of America. At its core, *The American Way of Death* was a manifesto by a Communist sympathizer against the world's great capitalist power: America was a land where the rabid profit motive inspired a group of citizens to wrench profits with unmitigated greed from the most vulnerable of targets—the dead and their survivors. "Much has been written of late about the affluent society in which we live, and much fun poked at some of the irrational 'status symbols' set out like golden snares to trap the unwary consumer at every turn," Mitford wrote in her introduction. "Until recently, little has been said about the most irrational and weirdest of the lot, lying in ambush for all of us at the end of the road—the modern American funeral." Mitford was a zealous consumer advocate of the far left out to nail scheming American businesses (she took on hospitals and doctors in a later book, *The American Way of Birth*). The only solution would be socializing the industry, which Mitford no doubt would have approved of. It is the same bottom line issue today for the consumer advocates and memorialites who condemn just about any thing the mortician does.

With Mitford's book, America had found a new whipping Boy—the "funeral men." *The American Way of Death* sparked a swarm of media coverage. *Time* and *Life* magazines followed Mitford with critical pieces and CBS broadcast a critical documentary called, "The Funeral Men." Prime time television contributed with a Halloween 1963 episode of *Dr. Kildare*, starring none other than the American funeral director, in the role of, "The Exploiters." Mitford's book also gave the memorialite movement a big push, enough to increase their numbers a bit and keep a lot of funeral directors on their toes. It also probably contributed to the rapid rise in cremation we've seen since 1970 and the eventual regulating of the funeral industry by the federal government.

Mitford was reportedly at work on a revision of her classic book when she died in the summer of 1996. She appeared in a recent BBC documentary, "Over My Dead Body," on the Americanization of the British death industry, where she can be seen grilling a British undertaker showing her his fine selection of caskets at the funeral parlor, and having tea with a friend in a cemetery, discussing the merits of socializing the business of death.

MORE SCANDALS

Today you can expect a few funeral and burial exposes each year on network tabloid shows and affiliates. NBC's *20/20* did a piece in November 1995 on pay-before-you-die scams. One involved a New Jersey mortician caught on hidden camera scheming with an undercover reporter to bilk the state out of funeral and burial money. The media never fails to find Death Industry scams to report. Because of the nature of the business the stories are inherently "sexy"—a word newspaper reporters use for the equivalent of very interesting—sexier than, say, a run-of-the-mill official-taking-bribe scandal. The *San Diego Union* reported in December 1995 that a mortuary charged with taking its sweet time tending to business let "bodies decompose" and kept cremains for months before giving them to survivors, or kept them for good instead of scattering them at sea like they were supposed to. In recent years, California has led the nation with cremation and cemetery scandals. At least three books and a score of articles have been produced as a result. Mass cremations, divvying out of commingled cremains, and the yanking out of dental gold and silver from to-be-cremated bodies have been common transgressions. Morticians are dragged into class-action suits in these cases for contracting with rogue crematories and cemeteries.

Newspapers across the country perform their role as consumer watchdog with articles warning readers to watch their wallets when entering the doors of the local mortuary. "Funeral's Price Can Be Somber," reads a January 1996 headline from the Tucson, Arizona, *Daily Star*, "Grief Stricken People Often Are Vulnerable." *The Press Telegram* of Long Beach, California, ran a series in the fall of 1995 called, "Death and Profits—The Crisis in the Cemetery Industry," in the wake of a scandal where gravediggers at one cemetery dug up about 3,000 human remains and tossed them in a pile behind a tool shed or in other graves to make room for new bodies so they could resell the graves. One "Death and Profits" article focused on mortuaries: "Planning ahead for the cost of eternity," reads the introduction, "The road from mortuary to cemetery is paved with gold—yours—if families aren't wary." *The Paper* of Monte Rio, California, wasted no time on subtleties in a subheadline for a March 1993 article: "Three decades after the publication of *The American Way of Death*, the funeral business remains a consumer hell." Standing in a photo topping the article is Karen Leonard, executive director of the Redwood Funeral Society and research assistant for none other than the queen of funeral muckraking, Jessica Mitford. The photo caption reads: ". . . Karen Leonard says her group can't recommend any local mortuaries."

Consumer's Digest, reaching about 1.5 million Americans, ran an extensive report in October 1995 titled, "Fraud in the Funeral Industry." It detailed what it believes is a free-for-all money-grab for America's billions of pay-before-you-die preneed dollars in this rapidly expanding funeral-insurance industry. Unlike most journalistic hits against morticians, *Consumer's Digest* went to the trouble of not condemning the entire industry:

". . . funeral and cemetery professionals are by and large skilled, honest and compassionate . . ." It also refers to the "death-care" industry, a euphemism used by many morticians unhappy with plain old funeral industry or the soberingly unflattering death industry. The piece is a bit soft in areas, settling for quotes from NFDA's handpicked spokesperson, and follows a pattern found in many newspapers covering the death industry: quoting the same experts in story after story who say pretty much the same thing. These experts include zealots who insist the industry is dominated by hopelessly greedy profiteers of death. These mortician mashers include Lisa Carlson and the Reverend Henry Wasielewski, founder of something called the Interfaith Funeral Information Committee, which has a World Wide Web site named, "Funerals and Ripoffs," seething with bad-faith condemnations of American morticians, a list of media exposes for perusal, and price lists of mortuaries in a given city showing huge disparities.

The *Consumer's Digest* article reports "about $50 million in preneed funds were stolen or reported missing nationwide," although this was not substantiated. The article bemoaned the lack of oversight in the preneed industry and suggested many of America's elderly are ripe for ripoff. Readers were warned about boiler room telemarketers working on commission, pitching pay-before-you-die policies to the elderly. It detailed a few scam stories where elderly folks gave their funeral dollars to crooked morticians who took them and ran or went out of business and ran. It referred to the "aggressively marketed [preneed] plans sold by multinational corporations," referring to the four publicly traded funeral-cemetery "consolidators."

But *Consumer's Digest* broke with the modus operandus of today's attack journalists who don't want their muckraking efforts diluted. Despite the specter of preneed horrors, we're told ". . . the vast majority of death-care firms are handling preneed funds honestly . . ." As usual, it's a few bad apples.

FUNERAL RULE

In 1984 the Funeral Rule became law. For the first time, the American funeral director would be regulated by the federal government. Mitford's book and the following media crusade had raised questions about this hush-hush industry. There were enough stories of grieving survivors exploited by opportunistic morticians to stir legislators on. Reverberations made their way to the chambers of Capitol Hill, and by 1972 the Federal Trade Commission began investigating how to regulate funeral directors. NFDA and other funeral associations fought it tooth and nail. When the Funeral Rule became law in 1982, NFDA appealed (and lost); National Selected Morticians, an invitation-only association, appealed to the Supreme Court (which refused to hear it).

Like any industry, morticians were opposed to government regulation in general, but the Funeral Rule, they believed, would turn their world upside down. They also couldn't understand why they had been singled out while the arch-rival cemetery industry had been left alone. When the law was passed they were able to get some provisions knocked out—like one forcing the funeral director to tell people prices over the phone, whether someone asked for them or not (making them come off as aggressive telemarketers).

A look at the rules of the Funeral Rule makes a layman ask: What was all the fuss about? The mortician is simply being asked to give funeral shoppers price lists and not lie to them about what they have to buy. Consider this summary of what the mortician must do under the Funeral Rule:

- Give customers three price lists when they come into the funeral home—one for caskets, one for outer burial containers—vaults and grave liners—and a general price list, which includes things like a basic service fee (usually $500 to $1,000), embalming (about $350), fees for using the mortuary for a visitation (about $700), etc.

- If someone calls and asks for price information, give it to them over the phone. Don't offer prices if they don't ask, unless you want to.
- Ask for permission to embalm—e.g., "Should we embalm your grandpa?" Don't even think of telling them grandpa must be embalmed, because the law says he does not have to be, unless the body is to be stored for more than a few days, at which time decomposition will probably be well under way, and the funeral home may not have a refrigerated morgue.
- Make sure the embalming-isn't-required explainer is written on your general price list; same goes for the casket-isn't-needed-for-a-cremation explainer; a cardboard box, the pseudo caskets discussed in Chapter two, or other alternative containers, as the government has designated them, will do.
- Don't charge a casket handling fee if someone buys their casket elsewhere and wants it delivered to your funeral home, as people do on occasion.

Twelve years of feisty congressional debate and this is what America got in the way of funeral home regulation. The reason it was such a big deal was many funeral directors were used to giving people one bill for everything, with little or no itemization. Your bill would be $4,000 and you'd have no idea half of it was for the casket, $500 for the vault, $300 for embalming, $500 for use of the visitation room, etc. The Funeral Rule has brought about the Great Unbundling, as the regulators call it, of the funeral bill.

Having to tell people embalming isn't necessary proved a particularly sore point: In the old days embalming was pretty much a given because most people had an open-casket wake, today's visitation. Grandpa had to look presentable, and the only way to do so before the body began to decompose, was to embalm, wax, and rouge. Once people are told grandpa doesn't have to be embalmed, the funeral and all the merchandise may be out the window—the casket and vault sale, the visitation fee, the whole ball of wax, as pointed out in the cremation casket video in Chapter two.

Enforcing the Funeral Rule is the Federal Trade Commission, the regulators who also monitor used car salesmen, credit rating agencies, and telecommunications companies. FTC started fining mortuaries in 1987 for Funeral Rule transgressions and to date has hit about seventy-five of them with fines totaling about $2 million. In early 1996 FTC's press office faxed out news to the trade press of a "Tampa Sweep." This referred to five Tampa area mortuaries nailed by FTC "test shoppers"—special agents posing as people shopping for funerals in sting operations. The funeral homes were charged with not giving out price lists, not saying there's no need to embalm, and other disclosure offenses. They all entered into consent decrees and agreed to pay fines and never break the Funeral Rule again. The highest fine was $35,000; one mortuary was fined nothing, as they were apparently financially impoverished, and under the Funeral Rule FTC cannot fine someone out of business. The other three were each fined several thousand dollars.

FTC's enforcement method of choice is the test shopper sting, although it also gets leads from competitors, customers, and disgruntled employees no longer working for the mortuaries they rat on. The stings are meant as a sober reminder to the mortician that the person browsing for caskets may be an impostor, a government spy dispatched to test the funeral director's Funeral Rule integrity. And so the temptation to tell customers that grandpa must be, say, cremated in a casket—and this $1,500 mahogany model over here may be just what you're looking for—is tempered with the consequences of an FTC hit. But chances of a government spy infiltrating American mortuaries is slim. FTC has its hands full enforcing wrongdoing in higher priority industries; Fed funeral test shoppers have been unleashed in just a few cities in a handful of states.

The most common Funeral Rule transgression is an act of simple neglect: not giving someone a price list, or having a price list that doesn't disclose what it's supposed to. Fines are based on the mortuary's annual gross revenue—the more they make the more they are fined. Most fines stay in the $10,000–$20,000 range, although the Tampa Sweep produced a $30,000 fine and Macias Mortuary Services in San Francisco was hit in January 1993 with a $60,000 fine for, according to FTC, "Failing to provide consumers with a casket price list or a statement of funeral goods and services they had selected."

FTC's Funeral Rule cause célèbre is its case against Stewart Enterprises, one of the publicly traded funeral-cemetery companies. Stewart owns about 200 mortuaries and 110 cemeteries, including about twenty-five mortuaries in Australia and five in New Zealand, and specializes in combination cemetery-mortuary operations. FTC says Stewart's five mortuaries in the Dallas/Fort Worth area gave out price lists with inadequate disclosures and committed other violations from 1984 until they were hit with a complaint in December 1991. Stewart had the complaint thrown out of federal district court on a technicality, but an appellate court overturned that decision. Stewart appealed to the U. S. Supreme Court, which refused to hear it. The parties were at square one in early 1996. FTC is asking the judge to fine Stewart $2 million and force the company to refund or rewrite thousands of preneed contracts that were sold to people who bought them using the alleged bogus price lists to make their decision. Stewart was trying to have the complaint thrown out again on another technicality.

The casket, the time-honored, sacrosanct merchandise of the funeral director, has in recent years been coveted by others who'd like a piece of the billion-dollar casket pie. In the old days, before the Funeral Rule, before jumping cremation rates, before Jessica Mitford and the rise of the memorialites, most funeral directors would have thought it virtually impossible for anyone to give the slightest consideration to buying caskets anywhere but the funeral home. But the good old days are gone. Strange as it sounds, in recent years people have been buying caskets at retail casket shops in California, Texas, Florida, Tennessee, and probably elsewhere. Family Heritage Casket Gallery in Memphis was doing a brisk business of a few dozen caskets a month in mid-1993 when I talked to the owner, Al Tacker, for an article I was doing on a lawsuit he filed against mortuaries and casket makers for allegedly colluding to knock him out of business. (Tacker told me he suffered a personal knockout when a casket maker punched him in the face during a confrontation at a casket plant.) When Russell Moore opened a strip mall casket store, Texas Casket Gallery in Mesquite, Texas, he got local and national press, as did Marti Frank, who opened the Direct Casket store in Los Angeles in late 1995.

Some people make their own casket, like an El Paso man who belonged to the defunct El Paso Memorial Society cooperative in the early 1990s. He used it, I was told by the former director of the society, as a bedroom chest until his final hour arrived. A pair of carpenters in Ashland, Oregon, make simple birch plywood caskets for Jewish burial societies, leaving middleman morticians out of the loop.

Funeral directors can lose casket sales to someone's preneed plan if it calls for a certain brand or model not offered at the mortuary serving the person when they finally die. Cemeteries can also be a source of casket competition, but not in Georgia and other states that limit the sale of caskets to funeral homes. Brunswick Memorial Park Cemetery in Brunswick, Georgia, challenged the mortician's monopoly on the treasured burial box when it started selling caskets in 1991. A year or so later, Brunswick was forced to stop after legislators sympathetic to the funeral lobby passed a law giving morticians exclusive casket-selling rights. Brunswick challenged the law but the State Board of Funeral Service, comprised of a majority of funeral directors, prevailed and Brunswick had to ship out its caskets (probably to the owner's other cemetery, where he'd recently opened a funeral home).

HANDLING FEE

With growing casket competition, many morticians were hoping to use the casket handling fee to penalize those bold enough to bring their own casket to the funeral home. But the Federal Trade Commission said no: If someone wants to bring their own casket to the funeral, so be it. No handling fee.

Casket stores and casket-selling cemeteries became a nuisance, if not a threat, to local morticians. The morticians complained to their state and national associations and NFDA was compelled to champion the cause of the casket handling fee. It was a vitally important symbolic issue to many. The raw cry of indignation goes something like: "The casket is our baby, we're the descendants of the cabinetmakers who started this industry, and we're the experts on funerals. Hands off!"

Two funeral association officials I discussed the handling fee with used restaurant analogies to get across their point that bringing your own casket to the funeral home was simply wrong. One of them, Bonnie Tippy, executive director of the New York State Funeral Directors Association (hired away from the Montana association in 1994) told me in an interview I did for *American Funeral Director*: "I doubt you could find one convention hotel facility in New York State that would allow the New York State Funeral Directors Association to bring in their own liquor for a cocktail party, and have them provide the bar men to pour the drinks. Are caskets really just a commodity? Or are they part of the service provided by a professional funeral director in providing for the full traditional service in all the many things they do?" NFDA counsel T. Scott Gilligan told me there was also the problem of liability: If the funeral director uses someone else's casket and the bottom drops out, they're likely to be liable.

The message to casket bandits is clear: Hands off, we're the professionals here; this is our merchandise, and only ours, to sell!

Not only does this line of reasoning say it is rude and tacky to bring your own casket to the funeral home, it also reminds those who don't understand what the big fuss is that a single foreign casket can throw a wrench into the mortician's pricing structure. The industry party line in this area, as espoused by NFDA, goes something like this: The price of the casket is figured into overhead costs; providing a funeral without revenue from the casket sale throws the pricing structure out of whack; the mortuary is guaranteed to lose money on that transaction. If it happens enough, other funeral shoppers are out of luck as funeral homes will have to raise overall prices to compensate.

FTC has heard this argument. It responds: Charge more for your basic service and come to terms with the reality that the casket is not a shoo-in with every customer you deal with. NFDA responds, "Don't tell us how to recover costs." In 1993 the association appealed the provision of the Funeral Rule forbidding the handling fee and lost.

Morticians and cemeterians have traditionally not gotten along, although there have been exceptions. A recent battleground pitting them against each other was Indiana—the state with the majority of the country's casket makers, and one of the highest average funeral bills. It began in 1989 when D. O. McComb & Sons Funeral Homes in Fort Wayne sued three cemeteries in federal court for the right to dig graves. This opening and closing, as digging a grave is called, is perhaps the most coveted and sacred rite of the cemeterian (it usually costs between $300 and $700). The ground is to the cemetery what the casket is to the funeral director. What could be more fundamental to a burial ground than digging a grave? And here was a funeral home suing to provide that service. It was the first suit of its kind.

McComb's legal argument focused on antitrust issues: The cemetery had no right to lock other parties out of providing a service. Where was it written, cried the plaintiff, that the cemetery had a monopoly on digging graves? McComb had an excavation company and was waiting for the case to end so it could start digging. The cemetery industry feared the case would set a precedent and tempt morticians everywhere to buy a backhoe or two and enter the grave-digging business. The American Cemetery Association, a rival of NFDA, contributed more than $100,000 to the defendant cemeteries' legal fees (and celebrated their eventual victory at its 1995 convention).

The defense was simple: We own this land and we have the right to choose who's going to perform the fundamental functions. Translation: Get your grubby backhoes outta our cemetery! Some said the suit boiled down to a feud between the owner of McComb and the owner of one of the cemeteries. Some said McComb was retaliating against the cemeteries for cutting into McComb's burial vault sales.

In the end, the cemeteries spent more than a million dollars on legal fees before the case was settled out of court in early 1995, with two of cemeteries' grave-digging rights intact; it was unclear if the third cemetery had stopped the rumble of alien backhoes.

Another recent development alarming morticians is the rise of the combination cemetery-mortuary. Usually they form when a cemetery builds a mortuary on its property. The first combo was established in 1933 when Forest Lawn Memorial Park in Los Angeles opened a mortuary. By the late 1970s, combos could be found throughout the country, and today there are several hundred.

The threat they pose to the stand-alone mortuary, as funeral homes are referred to when combos are discussed, is clear: People don't need them. If gas stations have become minimarts and chain drug stores now sell everything from cans of soup to underwear, why can't a cemetery sell everything you need when grandpa dies? Flowers? The flower shop is next to the funeral home. Headstone? Turn right at the crematory and check out the flat bronze markers behind the chain link fence. A religious service? Our quaint chapel seats 100, just what you're looking for. You'll need a vault—and we've got them, too.

Americans are always looking for convenience, so why not make death convenient? And so the cemeterians have.

6

LONG
LONESOME GRAVE

How Much Do Burials Cost? A lot.

—Death to Dust: What Happens to Dead Bodies

Americans don't reuse graves, like they do in much of Europe, where bones of the dead are dug out of cemetery plots and cremated or hauled off to an ossuary (a storage depot for this express purpose) when the lease on the grave is up and it's time to prepare it for someone else. Europe's practical burial strategies make it possible for cemeteries to stay active without worrying about increasing acreage, of which there's not much that people are willing to set aside for the dead. The situation in England is acute: It ran out of burial space following World War II. The obvious solution was embraced, and England's cremation rate has skyrocketed from single digits before the war to 70 percent today. But there

163

are still burial holdouts, and British burial authorities have tried to accommodate them. In London, a used grave can be used for a fresh burial after seventy-five years have passed, if survivors don't object or no survivors can be located. The remains—if any are left after decades or centuries in the ground—must not be disturbed, which means they stay in the grave now to be occupied by a fresh corpse. This, it seems, honors the sanctity of the grave while figuring the long-gone dead won't object.

Reusing graves sounds like a great idea to American cemetery strategist J. C. Redden, president of Cemetery Mortuary Consultants of Memphis and a forty-two-year veteran cemetery operator. In a book he wrote in 1993 on "money-making tips" for the death industry, Redden suggests: "How about renting [grave] space, and in thirty years cremating the remains and placing them in a wall niche? All of this you had arranged at the time of the first sale. Enough of that dreaming."

Redden is dreaming because in America the grave is protected by laws ruling they are sacrosanct and inviolable, and Redden's rental scheme would outrage more than a few citizens and politicians. Britain, a small island nation, was forced into a burial predicament from a growing population. America, still a land of vast, empty places, faces a burial crunch in some cities, but would anyone here except zealous cemetery sales people favor the radical, if not grisly, idea of renting graves? Our collective conscience on this matter might go something like this: You don't treat a grave as just another commodity to be wheeled and dealed. When the priest or rabbi or minister says ashes to ashes at the graveside, they mean the transformation is supposed to happen in the ground into which the casket's being lowered; this is an eternal thing, never meant to be a leasing arrangement after which remains are plundered for convenience and profit.

STACKED BURIALS

Saving space is a must for American cemeteries running out of land or unable to expand. Digging deeper than the familiar "six feet under" to make room for two, three, even four caskets stacked atop each other is one way the land is exploited. "Double-depth" burial, often husband and wife, is a popular choice these days. Gravediggers at one of America's most jam-packed burial grounds, Calvary Cemetery in Queens, New York, with nearly 2 million bodies in the ground, have often shoveled and backhoed nine feet down over the years to make way for three stacked bodies. The Mexicans have taken stacked burials to great depths. Two cemeteries in Monterey, Mexico—*Jardin Des Los Angeles* and *Jardin La Piedad*—bury as many as eight people to a single grave using the osario, a four-tier rack made of cinder blocks planted twelve to fourteen feet deep. The first body in is lowered to the ground-level tier. Five years later the bones are recovered from the coffin, bundled in a bag and placed in a little compartment or niche on the same tier, leaving room for another body. This process is repeated for each tier, for a net of two burials per tier, unless a person reserved for an occupied tier dies before the five-year decomposition period expires, at which time the new body occupies the second tier from the bottom, so the less-than-thoroughly decomposed body below it does not have to be removed. Even if people are dying less than five years apart, the least number of bodies in these space-saver tombs is four.

A Los Angeles cemetery dealt with land problems by stealthily digging up remains and reselling the graves. Over a twenty-year period, rogue gravediggers at Paradise Memorial Park in the suburb of Santa Fe Springs routinely exhumed human remains and dumped them (and the remains of caskets and headstones) in a pile behind a shed, or in other graves. The plundered graves were now ready for resale, and before long new bodies occupied them. When the story broke in the

summer of 1995, the L. A. *Times* reported that the man directing this twisted enterprise told investigators he didn't realize
what he was doing was illegal.

HISTORY OF AMERICAN CEMETERY

America's first burial crisis came in the late eighteenth century when churchyard and city graveyards were filled or filling
up. Many people condemned them as the source of yellow
fever and other diseases that periodically devastated the population with death and suffering. The cry went out over the land:
The dead must be carted out of here.

By 1831 the first rural cemetery, Mount Auburn, was laid
out in the woods outside Boston near Harvard College.
America had given itself a new euphemism for the land of the
dead, just as it would for coffins—the casket—by midcentury.
The word cemetery is derived from a Greek word for sleeping
chamber. The dead would now sleep in a rural park rather than
crammed in a nightmarish yard of graves that people avoided
like the plague. The rural cemeteries were a beautiful mix of
garden, shrine, museum, arboretum, nature preserve, and, of
course, a place to bury and entomb dead bodies. The woodland
was manicured by horticulturalists and rolled with valleys and
hilltops offering a glimpse of the city. There were ponds,
streams, mausolea, and Victorian artwork built by the country's
finest architects and artists. City guidebooks listed them as
must-sees. The cemetery was a place fit to honor the memory
of the dead. A place where the grieving souls of the living
would feel the soothing balm of nature. It was a pleasure to
stroll among these bucolic treats and architectural masterpieces. Visitors donned their Sunday best. Picnickers laid out
blankets under spreading chestnuts. Graffiti artists picked out
choice oaks. Rich folk toured the grounds in horse and buggy.

Hundreds gathered at chapel services. (And graverobbers found a new depot of fresh cadavers.) Other cities followed Boston's lead, and by midcentury America had established burial independence with these new rural cemeteries. We had more land than we knew what to do with; there was plenty of space for all of our dead.

By the late nineteenth century, cemetery entrepreneurs were developing a thriving burial and entombing industry that became as much the "American Way of Death" as embalming and caskets and funeral processions. In 1913 came the first memorial park, where the commercialization of the cemetery would reach its zenith. The basic idea was to squeeze as many graves out of the land as possible and sell them in advance. Cemeteries had been nonprofit entities; memorial parks were out to make a buck, just as any business was, so the cemetery itself was kept nonprofit and tax-exempt, as required by law, while separate corporations or joint stock companies worked as profit centers. With the land opened up in a great sweeping expanse, there were plenty of graves to sell: more burials, more grave markers, more dollars. Keeping the landscape and ornamentation simple kept labor maintenance costs down. Good old American ingenuity and frugality had arrived in the land of the dead.

Undertakers had established embalming, caskets, and viewing of the dead; memorial parks would bring us a burial ground transcending the traditional function of burial and entombment. They became the darlings of the burial scene, much to the credit of the first one, Forest Lawn in Los Angeles, which saw no reason not to be a cheerful place with plenty to do besides standing solemnly by a grave. Couples were married at Forest Lawn. Copies of Michelangelo's art were showcased. Admission was charged to see stained glass in the Great Mausoleum. And in 1933 Forest Lawn made history again when it opened a mortuary, making it the first one-stop-shopping death combo operation. Forest Lawn became a model for the twentieth century hustling cemeterian (and was the subject of two satirical novels). The memorial park was meant to be nonthreatening. The metaphor itself—"memorial park"—makes it clear this new burial ground was meant to lighten the Grim Reaper's sting, just as the rural cemetery had by placing the dead in manicured woodland. Graves in memorial parks lay in row after row on flat or gently rolling farm land, marked with simple flush markers. The landscape stretched unobstructed like a sweeping lawn without self-important in-your-face Victorian headstones and monuments and giant mausolea with sphinx and other ostentatious monuments outside reminding visitors this was indeed a land where the rich and famous dead made no bones about reminding you of the station they'd enjoyed in life. At the memorial park, whether well off or middle class, you got the same flat marker over your grave (often bronze). Selected statues and artwork were put in place here and there, not to honor any one individual, but as collective monuments to all the dead. A genuine great equalizer, this memorial park was said to be. The truth was different: Many of these exciting new burial grounds with the fancy name were exclusive clubs for whites until after World War II. In 1926 Forest Lawn went to the trouble of going to court (and winning)to rescind the burial contract of a black who had somehow bought a Forest Lawn grave plot without the powers-that-be knowing his race.

GRAVE PROSPECTOR CALLING

By 1935 there were about 600 memorial parks across the country with plenty of graves and merchandise to sell and plenty of people to buy them. In the trenches of the memorial park operation was the prospector—today more often called a memorial counselor. It was decided somewhere along the line that the best place to sell someone their grave was in the comfort of their home, and the prospectors were dispatched to the neighborhoods of America. They got leads and arranged to meet with a housewife at her home, or they'd pop in unexpectedly, just as the Avon Lady or traveling vacuum cleaner salesman might. Many worked on a commission-only basis; they sold graves or perished. The pitch was fairly simple and played on guilt and fear and an unburdening of one's conscience. It went: Everybody dies, no one likes to think about it, but if you don't make your burial arrangements ahead of time, you'll be placing a terrible burden on the ones you love when your final hour arrives.

The memorial park prospectors would carve out a huge new segment of the burial insurance business. The prospectors were the pioneers of today's pay-before-you-die preneed industry, although it was often called "before need" until the last twenty or thirty years. Besides tending to life's final chore before it was too late, buying before need saved you a bundle, promised the prospectors, because your grave would cost a bundle more if you were so inconsiderate as to leave it to your grieving widow to buy after you were gone—the old buy-now-or-pay-more-later line. Some prospectors gave Bibles to their mortal prospects to break the ice before starting their pitch, or as a gift to hold on to until they returned to meet with the husband, who usually held the purse strings. ("You're No. 1 Pre-Need Salesman: Heirloom Bibles, Heirloom Bible Publishers," reads an advertisement in the April 1971 *American Cemetery*.) Grave prospectors also carried maps and photos of the attractive memorial park they were working for, which the Joneses now had the opportunity to spend eternity in. If they closed a sale, they might return at a later date to sell "reloads," the grave markers, vaults and grave liners the Joneses would be needing.

Advertisements were used to drill home the bottom line. If people needed to be scared into buying their graves, then so be it. A before need advertisement, circa 1950, from a memorial park in upstate New York, shows two photos. One is "The Right Way" to buy a grave; one is "The Wrong Way." The photo on the left shows a middle-aged couple and three children gathered at a table in their home. They look on intently as a geekish-looking man sporting a polka dotted bow tie sits at the table and goes over a bunch of papers with a sharp-tipped pencil in hand. As you might have guessed, this is "The Right Way": Bring the whole family into the living room to buy mommy and daddy's graves from a salesman who dropped by from the local memorial park. Under the photo is the word "WISDOM," spelled vertically, with each letter starting the first word of a statement explaining why it's wise indeed to buy "Before Need." From the M evolves, "Money Saved at Today's Lower Prices," with the W offering this pearl of wisdom: "Wife and Husband Select Together."

The "Wrong Way" photo shows a disturbing scene out of a *Twilight Zone* episode. A young grieving widow stands at the cemetery on a dark and rainy day, an umbrella clasped in both hands, a young daughter by her side. Her face fearful, she stares gloomily into the ground. Across from her is a tall man in an overcoat. An authoritarian glare on his unforgiving face, he points a stern finger to the ground, signaling to an available grave for the recently expired husband who didn't have the good sense or consideration to buy one before he died. Where WISDOM prevailed in the living room, REGRET has descended on the cemetery. REGRET, too, is spelled vertically, and messages of fear encapsulate terse statements stemming from the first letters. The second R warns, "Ready cash is required for this emergency," while the first E brings, "Engulfed in Grief and Sorrow." And the T, summarizing this needn't-have-been tragedy, reads, "Thoughtless delay has proven costly."

Not everyone took such a harsh view of things. Although working the humor angle can be difficult in the pay-before-you-die business, it can be found, like in a 1971 print advertisement for

Rosewood Memorial Park in Tidewater, Virginia. "NOW YOU CAN ENJOY DIEING [sic]" goes the ad headline. "Call today for information about clean, dry, ventilated entombment at special preconstruction prices. $495/ single, $795/ two." The ad copy ends with a not-so-funny reminder: "Make arrangements for your mausoleum crypts now. You'll pay much more later." The ad was offensive enough to draw criticism from *Advertising Age* magazine, which said it was tasteless, and *American Cemetery*, which said it was an embarrassment to all the good folks out there burying the country's dead with respect and dignity.

Humor seems to have worked for Fred Donnell, an old-time grave prospector who started selling door-to-door in the 1950s, who is now owner of two cemeteries and a monument business in Rhode Island. I talked to Donnell and four other old-timer prospectors in 1993 for an "oral history of the memorial park," published in *American Cemetery*. Donnell remembers witty comebacks he had for all kinds of rejections: "People would say, 'I don't need to buy cemetery property; I'm going to be cremated.' My standard answer to that was, 'Oh, you're going to make an ash of yourself.' And they'd laugh." Donnell used the same logic for the cremation-minded that he used when selling a grave plot: Arrange for it now so loved ones aren't saddled with tending to this grim task. To he or she who would be cremated, Donnell would say: "'Now let me ask you another question: What are you going to do with the ashes?' And they'd say, 'Well, I'm gonna get cremated and scatter them.' 'Well,' I'd say, 'if you get cremated, you're not gonna scatter anything. You're going to ask your kids to take Daddy and throw him away, and they're not gonna do it. That's what's gonna happen. They're gonna do just what I'm trying to get you to do now, and they're gonna do it the hard way.'" The hard way meant "at-need," under duress, like the despondent widow and her child in the gloomy cemetery in the REGRET photograph.

Donnell nurtured a cadre of counselors who followed him

to the various memorial parks he worked at. He called this trusty crew Freddy's Rat Pack.

One of the more colorful characters was Al White, who started selling graves door-to-door in 1947 in Alberta, Canada. "A cemetery gypsy," White calls himself after forty years of selling graves and "reloads" across Canada and the U.S. (He retired in 1986 at Donnell's Rhode Island Memorial Park.)

White had more than a few tricks up his sleeve. In the early days, he traveled to homes with a thin attache case. Inside were Bibles, contracts, a receipt book, and a photo of his memorial park. The Bibles were gifts to women who told him when their husbands would be home so he could come back and pitch them together. (If he came back and the husband wasn't there, he'd ask for his Bible back.) White and his fellow pack rats called these appointments "sits," as in sitting down with the family in the WISDOM photo.

Like Donnell, White dished out a lot of guilt at his sits: "I'd tell someone, 'You wouldn't expect to talk about this with a relative, Mr. Jones. Wouldn't you prefer to talk to a complete stranger? Can you imagine you and your wife sitting at the table and having breakfast and one saying to the other, "Darling, it's such a beautiful day, let's go buy our graves today." Now, you're never gonna do that! There's only one time in your life when you're going to act, and that's when I'm sitting here talking to you. The only other time is when a death has occurred, when there's no ifs, ands, or buts, and you're gonna pay a fair fee. And you want to leave this burden to this sweet young lady sitting here?'"

Even when thrown out of a house, White would leave behind his message of die-smart-or-loved-ones-will-suffer: "I had one husband actually say to me, 'I wish she'd [the husband's wife] drop dead now. C'mon, get outta here. There's the door, now get out before I throw you out.' My reaction always was: 'The day will come that you will have thanked the good Lord for the fact that I was here, and that you got to act. But if you don't want to act, that's your loss, not mine.'"

When White had a taker, he tried making them think they'd been accepted into an exclusive organization: "Our close was always, 'Now we'll see if it's accepted by our company. If you'll be acceptable, you'll be notified by the company.' They never actually bought; it was the old negative close."

The 1950s were good years for White: "As the boom years hit it was like taking candy from a baby. Oh, it was beautiful. The graves had gone up to $100 apiece. We were financing ourselves and getting half of the down payment and half of the monthly payments. What they [had] started was the Gold Cross plan. You had to have been with the company at least two years. You'd set up appointments, a list of names was given to you in certain areas, of paid lot owners, and you went back to them and sold them their markers. We all made a good, decent respectable living."

PLUNDERING TRUSTS

Today's memorial counselors are out to lock in your death dollars, just as the prospectors were, and just like preneed morticians who want your preneed dollars in advance. Many cemeteries and memorial parks have sophisticated sales operations with telemarketers using leads to set up appointments for counselors. The International Cemetery and Funeral Association's (ICFA) convention and conference workshops are sprinkled with titles like "Sales Spectacular!" and "101 Ways to Generate Leads," to help the faithful pull in the preneed dollars. In March 1996, ICFA held an "International Sales Conference" at the Intercontinental in Miami, with cemeterians from South and Central America flying in for a few days of brainstorming. Meanwhile in Effingham, Illinois, the state cemetery association there was holding a "Sales Stimulator" at its spring meeting.

Inevitably, some grave-selling counselors take on the role of comforter to the people they're trying to sell. This doesn't always sit well with management. It's great to be compassionate, but not when it takes time away from the task at hand. At a cemetery convention workshop in 1995, J. Asher Neel, who runs Woodlawn Memorial Park in Orlando, Florida, reminded a gathering of 100 that counselors were there not just to comfort grieving widows but to sell preneed. J. C. Redden, the consultant dreaming of renting graves, has no place for cemetery counselors digressing to the realm of social worker. In his book on tips for making money—which, for the record, is titled, *The Best and the Rest of Redden's Rules of Thumb: Almost 200 Money-Saving, Money-Making Tips for the Cemetery/Mortuary Industry*—Redden warns of the "pitfalls of the family service approach," with family service being the compassionate wing of the cemetery sales effort. "In the first place," he writes, "the pre-need division resents the family service approach. That having been said, another pitfall is family service people tend to become social workers. Their service motive and case load frequently prevent much in the way of pre-need sales volume. Even those people who start out fast to produce revenue in preneed sales through family service, tend to tail off as their case loads increase. Social workers do not write contracts. Family service people lose sight of the fact that the greatest aid they can render a family is to sell them."

Among Redden's nearly 200 questions are touchy ones, like how to "get rid of the oldtimer," and the blander, "How much cash should pre-need sales bring in?" His book clearly shows that many cemeteries are bottom-line businesses with owners who want—what else?—to make lots of money. ICFA's monthly magazine, *Cemetery Management,* has a "Sales & Marketing" column with tips for guys and gals on the front lines. In the February 1996 column, cemetery sales pro Robert A. McConneghy III gave some tips on "Closing." The tips are directed to "people who never were in sales [to] feel comfortable in asking for the order." On how to "develop the emotions of the family," McConneghy writes: "In our presentation, we must 'back the hearse up to smell the flowers.' There are many ways to do this, but one of the most effective ways is to remove the husband from the picture and take the widow on a death shopping spree." Clearly there's no time for sentimentality when a sale is at stake. ". . . the emotion of profit or greed helps create urgency," explains McConneghy in his recapitulation of the old line about buying your grave now or paying a bundle later. Be sure, however, you don't get caught in a lie: "Make certain that any claims you make regarding price increases can be substantiated."

With a lusty profit motive alive and well in the burial/entombment business, it shouldn't come as a surprise that there's been more than a handful of plundered cemetery perpetual care funds. These are pools of money comprised of a percentage of a given cemetery's pay-before-you-die dollars. Requirements vary from state to state. Some require the money to go in trust or endowment funds, passbook savings accounts, or other safe investments. Some states pool all this money together as one giant endowment fund. The people running Paradise Memorial Park, the Los Angeles cemetery reusing graves, were charged with embezzling hundreds of thousands of dollars from its perpetual care funds. Shortly after this story broke, two other Los Angeles burial grounds—Hollywood Memorial Park and Lincoln Memorial Park—were also charged with siphoning hundreds of thousands of dollars from their trusts. A year earlier, a Long Beach cemetery had been charged with the same offense. These stories opened a can of worms for California's cemetery industry. It had been just a few years since the California cremation scandals (burning bodies en masse, extracting gold and silver from teeth, etc.) and now it was the hour of reckoning for cemeteries. It was clear the three-man regulatory board responsible for keeping tabs on about 200 California burial grounds and trust funds worth hundreds of millions of dollars was sorely inadequate. The board was disbanded, and the State Consumer Affairs Department took over regulatory chores.

Illinois had its own cemetery trust fund horror show. The State Comptroller, Loleta Didrickson, vowed to track down the swindlers who allegedly "plundered" $3.8 million from trust funds at bankrupt Forest Home Cemetery in Springfield. A February 1996 *Chicago Sun-Times* article includes a photo of Didrickson standing by a freshly dug grave at Forest Lawn that would not be receiving a body any time soon because the money to pay for burying it was nowhere to be found. The headline reads: "Cemeteries Face Controls—State Comptroller Aims to End Fraud in Burial Trust Funds."

MOVING THE DEAD

When bodies go in the ground in American soil, it's supposed to be forever: body to bones, bones to ashes, ashes to ashes, dust to dust, in perpetuity. With a few exceptions, the hundreds of millions of Americans buried over the centuries have been left in the ground, and for those who aren't yet dust, their remains will likely stay put. But things do come up, like the grave plundering at the Los Angeles cemetery—and the fairly common practice of moving burial grounds.

Graveyard transplants usually happen in the name of Progress: The dead and their tombstones are evicted to make way for highways, condos, airports, town halls, and so on. In the seventeenth, eighteenth and early nineteenth centuries, U.S. graveyards often stood in the center of town, next to the church or near the village green. How could these God-fearing folks have known that their dead would be in the way as the population of cities mushroomed and the industrial revolution wrought urban sprawl?

From 1857 to 1880, about 10,000 dead were moved from small churchyard burying grounds to Calvary Cemetery in Milwaukee. Get-the-dead-outta-here sentiment gathered steam in San Francisco in the early twentieth century as leaders of the prospering city could no longer tolerate the cemeteries, which had become revolting eyesores. Weeds and brush scoured the landscape, vandals toppled tombstones, and bones from shallow graves lay scattered about. One of the more graphic reports told of kids playing kickball with skulls. By about 1900, the city had banned burials altogether, and when thousands of mausoleum tombs were destroyed in the 1906 earthquake, the momentum to rid the city of the dead picked up. And so the evictions began. From the 1890s to the 1940s, tens of thousands, if not hundreds of thousands, of the dead and their headstones were moved out of San Francisco. Many were carted to railroad cars and delivered ten miles away to Colma, America's most famous cemetery town (seventeen of them, one for pets) with 1,100 inhabitants and about a million dead. Calvary Cemetery moved 39,000 remains to a mass grave at its new cemetery, Holy Cross, at Colma. Thousands of graves, including many of paupers and Chinese immigrants, were never moved from burial grounds in what is now San Francisco's Lincoln Park.

The graveyard transplant in Thomaston, Connecticut, occurred in 1882. Town leaders hired a teamster with oxen and laborers to cart away the stones and bones to make way for a red-brick town hall and opera house. A handful of God-fearing townsfolk objected to what they saw as pure desecration, but the majority prevailed and the burial ground was moved a half-mile away to a patch of sloping woodland, where today you'll find 100 headstones shaded under towering pine trees at the end of a path of pine needles next to Thomaston's Hillside Cemetery. Today some Thomastonians swear the opera house is haunted by the ghosts of those who once rested under this hallowed ground, bringing to mind the movie *Poltergeist*, where tormented spirits trapped in a buffer zone between the living and the dead terrorize a family living in a house built on a graveyard that was supposedly moved (they moved the head-stones but not the remains).

Churches over the years have sometimes delegated care of their burial grounds to others. This usually happened because the congregation didn't have workers to maintain them, or they were going out of business from a dwindling congregation. So away they went, tombstones and all, to a bigger, better burial ground. Woodlawn Cemetery in the Bronx, New York, a sprawl-ing 400-acre property with 1,000 mausolea, has received twelve transplanted church graveyards over the years (as well as the members-only plot of the New York YMCA and other pri-vate graveyards).

100,000 BURIAL GROUNDS

The practice of moving burial grounds continues today. It's not unusual for old headstones clustered in the woods or settled in a ravine to be in the way of a developer's bulldozer. No one knows the number of burial grounds scattered across America, but a common estimate is 100,000. This includes about 25,000 known entities, including 10,000 memorial parks and municipal and private cemeteries; 7,500 Catholic cemeteries; and a smattering of burial grounds for Jews, Chinese, Muslims, African-Americans, Native Americans, and others.

The 75,000 unknowns include thousands of family and vil-lage plots, long ago abandoned, laid out from the earliest days of the New England colonies through the first half of the twen-tieth century. A burial ground can be two graves on a farm dug by kinfolk laying Ma and Pa to rest in the earth where they toiled their years away. It can be a handful of slate markers at the graves of colonists killed by Indians, buried where they fell.

An abandoned Indian burial ground on the grounds of a camp razed by pioneers. A forgotten African-American graveyard tucked on the outskirts of a cemetery that refused to bury blacks. A "Boot Hill" cemetery in the West holding the remains of slain gunfighters and train robbers. A potter's field, where outcasts, homeless, and the poor were laid in whatever patch of earth could be found.

Sometimes developers discover these forlorn graves during excavations. A laborer with a spade shoveling dirt at a construction site bangs into something hard and it turns out to be a stone bearing an inscription. Further digging reveals it's one of a handful of tombstones. Protocol usually calls for trying to track down survivors of the dead with a public notice in the newspapers. The burial ground may be 300 years old, but the sanctity of the grave and state and local laws governing the dead call for next of kin, if any are to be found, to have a chance to claim remains. When the moving has been sanctioned— usually by a court—individual remains, if any are found, are to be moved and reburied, with corresponding headstones or markers placed over them. How diligently grave movers stick to this protocol is anyone's guess.

Sometimes historical groups and native Americans block burial ground transplants. A controversy stirs in the local papers and the bulldozers are called off. In November 1995, the Matinecock Tribal Nation was rallying to save an ancestral burial ground at the Fort Totten military base in Queens, New York, which was to be closed down, with talk of clearing it out for development. In September 1995, the *Herald-Tribune* of Sarasota, Florida, reported that officials had set aside money to protect "Centuries-old Indian [burial] mounds" on a place called Snead Island in Manatee County.

Sometimes progress outweighs considerations of respect for the dead (after all, it's the developer's land). A huge transplant came during 1993 and 94 at Washington Park Cemetery in St. Louis—3,000 graves schlepped away to make room for the MetroLink rail line. Developers aren't finished; in 1996, another 9,000 graves and corresponding remains were to be moved from Washington Park to provide visibility for a runway at Lambert Field.

DISINTERMENTS

Another way the dead end up somewhere other than where they were laid to rest for eternity: disinterments—when individual remains are dug up and moved. This usually happens when a survivor is moving and wants the remains of a loved one to come along. Sometimes detectives get court orders to exhume remains as part of their gathering of evidence in murder cases. Serenity Gardens Cemetery in Mobile, Alabama, does five or six disinterments a year. Everything's handled at the local level. When a removal request comes in, Serenity fills out an "application for disinterment" and sends it to the Bureau of Vital Statistics at the County Board of Health office. In graves without vaults, with the body in a wood casket, all that's usually left—unless it's a recent interment or the body had a thorough embalming—are bones, a skull, a burial suit or gown, pieces of casket, perhaps some jewelry, and a few trinkets tossed by loved ones on top of the casket. If the body is in a vault, as opposed to within the slabs of a concrete grave liner, the vault is smashed open and the casket is hoisted out and delivered to its new home. (Here's where vault makers earn reputations.) Serenity Gardens also receives disinterments. A recent arrival: the "casketed" remains of an elderly man, dead for four years, shipped in from Florida after his widow moved to Mobile. "She wanted his remains here so she could visit his grave and put flowers there," explained Serenity manager Glenda Bullard, whose father's bones were reinterred in her cemetery in the late 1960s after she took the reigns.

Another threat to the peace of the grave—the grave robber,

still among us, although better described today less as a body snatcher than a skull-and-bone thief, unearthing graves or rifling mausoleum crypts to snatch a bone or two for devil worship, bragging rights, or a drunken morbid thrill. Many nabbed raiding cemeteries are young males in some state of altered consciousness. Natural disasters also disturb the dead, like floods in 1993 and 1994 washing out cemeteries in Hardin, Missouri, and Albany, Georgia. Hundreds of the dead were washed downstream, some bobbing on the waters undisturbed in trusty caskets.

RECLAIMING GRAVES

Cemeteries sometimes find themselves with abandoned burial plots. This is often seen as an opportunity to repossess coveted burial space. Someone may have bought a dozen graves as a family plot a century ago; six bodies were buried and now there's six empty graves. But neither the owner nor heirs are to be found, or they're all dead and buried (or cremated) elsewhere. Whether cemeteries may reclaim abandoned graves depends on what state they are in. Wisconsin says yes, the graves are yours after forty years have passed since the plot was purchased, and the cemetery has made a reasonable effort to track down heirs. In Michigan it's up to local governments to decide if municipal cemeteries (700 of them in Michigan) can reclaim forgotten graves. For Michigan's 140 for-profit cemeteries, the decision goes to a circuit court judge.

New York cemeteries have no such luck. The plot, whether abandoned or not, is protected by a state law granting an "inalienable" right of the grave itself not to be disturbed, reclaimed, resold, donated to charity, or whatever. A plot could have been bought 150 years ago, the heirs are all dead, but the land must sit there unoccupied. New York's cemetery lobby has tried in recent years to convince legislators to pass a bill that would strike down this law. One reason they've failed is that state legislators championing consumer rights suspect cemeterians might not search as long and hard as they should in their repo efforts to find rightful plot owners. (Imagine the horror when the owner of a grave returns to find a stranger's body in it.) Especially eager to reclaim fallow graves are cemeteries in New York City, where burial space is scarce and sold at a premium. (Diehard New Yorkers with reasonable burial budgets can find plenty of space in Westchester County and Long Island.) Woodlawn Cemetery in the Bronx, the receiver of the transplanted church graveyards, figures it could reclaim land for thousands of new burials if the bill passes.

Abandoned grave plots are one thing, unwanted plots are another. Somebody living thousands of miles from the cemetery where great-grandpa bought a family plot 100 years ago may have no burning desire to have their bodies flown back to rejoin the clan for eternity when their time comes. Some may still be in town but have decided to be cremated and have no use for this little chunk of real estate they own. Some simply want the cash the cemetery is willing to pay for the "interment rights" of the grave. Some people will settle for a swap: They exchange their unwanted plot for one in a favored cemetery. Helping out in transactions like these is the ICFA through its lot exchange program.

Some states let cemeteries buy back interment rights, but, alas, New York cemeteries are again out of luck in this area. The stodgy law forbidding the reclaiming of abandoned plots also forbids the reselling of them. Woodlawn's buy-back candidates include the YMCA plot (mentioned earlier), only half filled with 140 burials. The Y apparently doesn't have anyone requesting burial in its communal plot and would just as well have the cash Woodlawn is willing to pay for the unoccupied section.

BURIAL CRUNCH

A bit of a burial bloat has befallen some of our urban cemeteries, like those in metropolitan New York, scraping for land and charging a premium for what's left. At the same time, there's plenty of space in the ground at cemeteries in many of our large population centers. Rose Hills Memorial Park in Los Angeles, the largest burial ground in the country, has 2,500 acres, of which 1,900 are undeveloped. So even with about 9,000 dead arriving here each year, there's room for a few million or so more bodies. Spring Grove Cemetery in Cincinnati, at 740 acres, has land for another century or so of burials. Where space is a problem is at crowded cemeteries in areas where the local community says no to expansion, or the cost of buying new land is prohibitive. A cemetery that wants to expand faces the same obstacles a developer may face when planning a factory, or a city proposing, say, a sewage treatment plant: Who wants one in their backyard? When zoning boards are presented with a choice between a shopping mall or a cemetery expansion for a coveted piece of town real estate, which do you think gets the nod?

So space-strapped cemeteries are using a mix of space-saving strategies to stay active with current property. Some rummage through the grounds looking for spots that might never have been considered. Rocky woodland is cleared. Roads are torn up and re-landscaped. Body-stacking in multiple depth graves is not uncommon. Wind Ridge Cemetery in Cary, Illinois, buries people in the woods on a hilltop overlooking a lake. They call this land of the dead au natural Woodland Trail, the trail being a path sprinkled with wood chips. No headstones or statues or neatly cut lawns here. Graves are marked with boulders sporting name plaques. Cremains are embedded in stone walls. "When a tree falls in the middle of this place, it stays," explains cemetery consultant Larry Anspach (whose clients include the Mexican cemeteries using the multitiered osario).

LET DEER DO THE MOWING

Taking back-to-nature burial to the extreme is Bruce J. Morgan, an "environmental designer/naturalist" from Archer, Florida. Morgan calls himself a waterfall specialist, and says his company, Environmental Design, builds biosphere reserves in parks and hotel atriums. Now he wants to build them in cemeteries. I met Morgan, a short man with a brown afro and wire rim glasses, in October 1995 at the American Cemetery Association expo in Cincinnati. On display at his booth was a miniature tropical rain forest. He told me about a recent excursion he'd made to a cave deep in a South American rain forest and how he'd been spending a lot of time lately looking for rare plants in caves in exotic locales. His pitch to the cemeterians: I can turn your staid landscape into an exotic paradise, a beautiful botanical garden preserve with plenty of room for hiking, jogging, fishing—anything people do these days in invigorating outdoor settings; people will flock in droves.

"Let deer do the mowing in summer, and a carpet of autumn leaves cover the graves in winter," Morgan wrote in a grant proposal to philanthropist George Soros, who is funding a program of death education called Project on Death in America. "Dandelions are always welcome," in Morgan's burial park. "Let a stately oak, or perhaps a grouping of boulders in a field of wildflowers, serve as monuments for those of us who wish to return something to the earth. Every family that obtained membership in such a park would not only gain access to a vast tract of open land for recreation, but would also contribute to the protection in perpetuity of one of our last wild places." Morgan's scheme would call for a weeding out of the American Way of Death. He sounds like Jessica Mitford when taking a crack at morticians: "By custom or by law, our corpses are often poisoned with formaldehyde, dressed 'as though for a funeral,' put on public display and subjected to nauseating platitudes, hermetically sealed into a casket, then buried in serried ranks in sterile cemeteries that are routinely violated with herbicides, pesticides, and lawn mowers. After that we are forgotten. The cost of all this is almost as outrageous as the insult."

Soros turned down his proposal, and when I last talked to Morgan in March 1996 he was still trying to land his first cemetery account.

MAUSOLEA

The new workhorse of the American cemetery is the community mausoleum. Thousands of these houses of the dead for the masses populate our burial grounds. Huge mausolea are going up in population centers across the country. Ten thousand crypts await the dead at Gate of Heaven Mausoleum in East Hanover, New Jersey, a project of the Roman Catholic Archdiocese of Newark, completed in 1995. Under construction in Clearwater, Florida, at Sylvan Abbey Memorial Park, is Peacefield Mausoleum. When completed in a few years, Peacefield's crypt count will be 15,000 (with 6,500 niches for cremains). Six stories of crypts fill Towers of Peace Mausoleum at Lauderdale Memorial Park Cemetery in Fort Lauderdale.

Along with the mausoleum boom has come the rise of the columbarium—the home of cremains. While some scatter cremains, as detailed in Chapter four, many bury or inurn them. "Niches" may be in a "free-standing" wall of granite, marble, or concrete, plunked down in the middle of an unremarkable cemetery. They can be ornate wood shelves in an elegant room. They can be entire walls within a mausoleum adorned with "niche front" mosaics and artwork. The "Cremorial" columbarium unit by Matthews International, a publicly traded manufacturer of monuments and cremation equipment, is a rectangular wall that looks like a condo's community mail box structure meant strictly for packages. The "Cremorial III" is a family columbarium with eight niches lining a marble altar topped with a bronze eagle. A platform of Matthews bronze niches within a brickwork island of small bushes is another columbarium design. A company called Permacrete makes a little wall of "Modulum niches . . . ideal profit-makers for wall exteriors, stand-alone banks, fountain walls, walkway railings, and benches," says Permacrete ad copy.

Old-style columbaria are entire buildings, or a series of rooms within a building. One of the most remarkable is at Fresh Pond Crematory in Queens, New York, built in the early 1880s, where about 50,000 urns occupy 20,000 niches. Fresh Pond has twenty separate columbarium sections, including the Old Chapel, which looks like it could be the office of an Ivy League university president. A Tiffany stained-glass skylight filters hues on lavender walls of arched niches framed in bronze and plaster-of-paris. This was one of Fresh Pond's earliest rooms, and the cremains and memorabilia of rich and eccentric New Yorkers of the early twentieth century are here. Each niche holds one or more urns. Most are bronze, silver or gold; some are shaped like jugs, some square boxes. Photos, medals, busts, and whatever mementos survivors thought fitting (and would fit) crowd the urns.

A handful of construction firms, architects, and artists specialize in mausolea and columbaria, and since the end of World War II they have carved out a busy niche for themselves. Hundreds are built each year at memorial parks and cemeteries across the country. They appeal to the cemeterian because they are the most efficient use of land for laying away the dead, even more than graves at flat open memorial parks and the stacked burial method. Today's community mausoleum is the idea of the Mexican *osario* merged with architecture: The dead are slid in their caskets into rectangular crypts stacked in tiers within the walls of buildings. (This is called entombment as opposed to the more precise encryptment, rarely if ever used.) The most expensive crypts are in the middle tier because survivors are face-to-face with the remains of loved ones. There's no bending, stooping, or reaching involved. If your loved one is in tier six or seven, fifteen or twenty feet up, you'd best bring a stepladder or borrow the cemetery's hydraulic "casket lift" if you want to touch the shiny marble or granite crypt front.

Mausolea have been described as warehouses for the dead, an unsympathetic view considering many are imaginatively designed, graced with marble and granite walls and floors, and elegant furniture decorating posh foyers. You'll find skylights, mosaics, and stained glass windows; statutes, monuments, and artistic trimmings of all design; chapels, courtyards, and columbarium walls. Mausolea can be long, nondescript pillboxes or stylized according to the whims of the cemetery or architect, like Our Lady of Angels Mausoleum at San Carlos Cemetery in Monterey, California, completed in 1994, built in the Mission style seen everywhere in California, with red terra-cotta roof tile and courtyard gazebo.

People don't object to proposed mausolea like they do to cemetery expansions. With mausolea, cemeteries usually don't have to worry about battling angry residents at zoning board meetings and spending thousands on attorneys and consultants to present their case for burying more bodies in town. The mausoleum is on cemetery grounds, so proposals usually sail through town approvals. For less than a million dollars, a cemetery can build a mausoleum with 1,000 or so pricey crypts, which can be sold preneed just like graves. A working formula for a cemetery constructing a mausoleum is $750 per crypt. Mausoleum crypts—as opposed to the above-ground garden and lawn crypts—are generally priced from a few thousand dollars to $10,000 each. It's more expensive to be interred in a building, for one, because of maintenance costs. Quite gruesome problems can surface, like stinking bodies (a bad embalming, a leaky casket) dripping a putrid mix of embalming chemicals and body fluids (despite liners meant to catch this postmortem muck), and the Phorid fly, which feeds on decomposing humans. Companies that make mausoleum maintenance products refer to these ill-mannered corpses as stinkers and leakers. And there's electricity, cleaning, and other costs found with the care of any building.

KING CRYPT

America's reigning King Crypt is Inglewood Park Cemetery in Los Angeles. Inglewood was having trouble with local authorities getting expansion plans approved, so they've looked to the crypt to keep business robust. When Inglewood's Sunset Mission mausoleum is complete in a year or so, it will have about 30,000 crypts, bringing Inglewood's tally to more than 100,000 crypts and niches in a dozen or so mausolea, including several thousand under a parking lot in a den of catacombs called Capistrano Gardens (no visitors without an escort). Despite California's high cremation rate, there are plenty of pockets with burial holdouts, especially in areas with lots of hispanics, a predominantly traditional Catholic group, more often than not giving cremation a thumbs down. Inglewood's subterranean Manchester Garden mausoleum, completed in 1995, has 28,000 crypts in seven underground and two aboveground levels; an elevator shuttles visitors to the floor of their loved one's space in the wall.

A BRIEF HISTORY OF THE MAUSOLEUM

All these crypts wouldn't be in place if Americans weren't buying. The same zeal of the "before-need" grave-seller is in place at cemeteries building mausolea. Gate of Heaven in New Jersey sold 5,000 crypts before the building was finished; this helped out nicely with the financing.

Those buying are those who can't bring themselves or loved ones to be cremated but who also don't like the thought of being in the ground. Perhaps these cryptonites, as you might call them, feel they have cheated death a bit by not decomposing as rapidly as their brethren in the ground: many mausoleum bodies, stuck in a casket in a wall, end up hard and leathery, like a mummy. Maybe it's the thought of being inside rather than out. The loved one can be visited in the warm and shiny marble confines of the mausoleum whether it's raining or twenty degrees below zero. The mausoleum is not an American or European invention. It can be traced to 353 B.C., when the wife (and sister) of Mausolus of Halicarnassus, ruler of Caria in Asia Minor, built a huge fortress tomb for him when he died. Hundreds of statues sprouted off this sprawling five-story structure. It was "surrounded by a colonnade of thirty-six columns [supporting] a pyramidal superstructure receding in twenty-four steps to the summit. On the top was a four-horse chariot of marble," according to architecture historian Howard Colvin. "By fusing tall podium, temple columns and pyramidal roof into one, the designers of the Mausoleum had created a new architectural formula for the glorification of the dead." Nothing like the Mausoleum of Halicarnassus had been seen before. It became one of the Seven Wonders of the Ancient World and was eventually sacked by stone robbers and treasure seekers, and much of it is believed to have been destroyed by an earthquake.

The Greeks were impressed with the Mausoleum of Halicarnassus and began building their own mausoleion, as they called them, coining a name for this new house-tomb. The Romans followed suit and the mausoleum evolved into a staple of the architecture of antiquity. It remained the burial space of choice for the rich and powerful—as well as some common

Romans banding together for communal mausolea—until the rise of Christianity. The Roman Catholic rank and file rejected mausolea, opting for strategically placed entombment in church and cathedral tombs and vaults (the closer to the altar, the better the odds of a quick entry through the pearly gates.) The mausoleum, although still found here and there, especially in the pagan north, fell out of favor for more than a thousand years.

The Reformation set the stage for a comeback. Protestants rejected the Catholics' belief that souls could be inched toward heaven by prayers and choice church burials. "But," writes Colvin, "to be buried in a mausoleum that stood on its own without any provision for regular religious services was more than a gesture of aristocratic privilege or of neoclassical taste: It implied a new attitude towards the afterlife which was at variance with a thousand years of Catholic belief and practice." The British Isles led the way, and by 1700 new mausolea appeared in churchyards there. In 1729 the first major mausoleum off consecrated ground was built at Castle Howard in Yorkshire, a huge domed fortress with Romanesque columns. By the late eighteenth century mausolea could also be found in Germany and Sweden.

WASPS in America looked to their brethren overseas for inspiration for the mausolea they were erecting in the new rural cemeteries. Catholic and Jews did the same, but the grandest (and most expensive) are found in the nonsectarian cemeteries. Huge and elegant as some of our contemporary mausolea are, few compare to America's great mausolea, built from the mid nineteenth through the early twentieth centuries. The rich wanted to outdo each other with great structures of granite, marble, stone, and bronze. (Some were built with the added purpose of thwarting graverobbers.) Top architects were hired, like James Renwick, whose work includes New York's St. Patrick's Cathedral. Americans with the desire (and money) to go out in grandiose style erected Gothic domes and drums, Greek temples, Egyptian Revival pyramids, and various neoclassical, Art Deco, Moderne, and other styled mausolea. Renaissance chapels, the Parthenon, and Egyptian temples appeared. Bronze angels and pharaohs graced mausoleum doors. Tiffany stained glass windows were common. An unsubtle stretch of domes, temples and miniature cathedrals unfolded to become Millionaire's Row at Oakland's Mountain View Cemetery. A pair of Sphinx knelt outside F. W. Woolworth's (the department store magnate) Egyptian temple mausoleum. Gargoyles protruded from eaves at the canopied sarcophagus tomb of the "Soda Fountain King" at Brooklyn's Green-Wood Cemetery. Meatpacker Herman Armour's Gothic mausoleum was made of pink granite and topped with a bronze dome.

Today's burial crunch is really not a crunch. There's plenty of space for the dead, but a lot of people in some cities don't want it opened up for burial. Meanwhile, the number of dead headed into the ground will gradually dwindle into the twenty-first century everywhere but parts of the Bible Belt and rural areas because of cremation's rapid rise and the mausoleum movement. Even with a huge growth in deaths starting in thirty or forty years as baby boomers start dying in large numbers, the traditional American grave will become lonely indeed.

7

ON THE FRINGE

Leading the crusade to teach Americans about their right to tend to their dead is fifty-eight-year-old Lisa Carlson of Hinesburg, Vermont, author of *Caring for Your Own Dead*, published in 1987, five years after she delivered her first husband to the crematory after he shot himself to death on a snowy winter's night. Like the two Toms of the direct cremation movement, she has contempt for the traditional American funeral director and lays out in her book how people can avoid them entirely by taking care of the details themselves, from cleaning and dressing the body, to delivering the body to the crematory or cemetery, to digging a grave. In most states, you can do these things if you go to the trouble of getting documents like a burial transit permit, the death certificate, and various disposition authorization forms. The funeral director can be left completely out of the loop, although some states require a mortician to conduct or at least be present at postmortem services. If you're burying your own in New York State, for instance, the mortician must be there.

"If you wanted to bury grandpa on a farm in upstate New York," says Carlson, "you'd have to have a funeral director around, even if he's standing behind a tree." Carlson says handling your own dead, as many Americans did in their homes as recently as the early twentieth century, is "a logical extension of the hospice movement," which has spawned groups across the country in the past twenty years or so helping people die at home. Most hospice nurses exit when the person dies and calls in the mortician.

Carlson's book created a bit of a national stir and she found herself on the *Phil Donahue Show* and *Good Morning America*. She started getting letters from people across the country inquiring about this extreme form of self reliance and eventually took the reigns of Vermont's death cooperative, the Memorial Society of Vermont, and emerged as spokesperson and leader of what you might call America's do-it-yourself death movement. In June 1996 she became executive director of the Funeral and Memorial Societies of America (FAMSA), the umbrella memorialite organization for the 140 death cooperatives, discussed in Chapter four.

Carlson follows in the footsteps of the unrelentingly anti-mortician social crusaders, a-la Jessica Mitford. She sees Everyman Funeral Director as a scheming money-grubber determined to sell expensive caskets. There is no good to be found in what they do. The average American has been bamboozled into thinking otherwise. Redux *The American Way of Death*.

A SUICIDE, A BOOK, A CRUSADE

How Carlson, became a do-it-yourself death crusader begins with personal tragedy. Like many memorialites, a combative encounter with a funeral director launched her to a career as advocate for those shopping for life's final purchase. Her story begins at her home at 2:30 A.M. on a winter's night in 1981. She woke and found that her thirty-one-year-old husband, John Brackett, was not by her side. She went outside and followed his footprints in the snow to his pickup truck at the end of the driveway. He had shot himself in the stomach with his hunting rifle.

John had been suicidal. He tried to kill himself once a few years back with an overdose of Sominex. He had talked about killing himself since Carlson met him when he was twenty-seven or twenty-eight years old. He was legally blind and prone to depression, yet despite this and his suicidal tendencies Carlson says he taught first grade at the local elementary school. Carlson, eleven years younger than John, says she married this troubled man—"an unbelievably sensitive person," in her words—because she loved him: "He was a walking Jesus, just a wonderful man." When she found John dead in the truck, she called the police and started calling funeral directors.

Carlson and John didn't have much money; she was a housewife and struggling freelance writer, and John's teaching salary wasn't much. Cremation was the way to go, and Carlson wanted to bring John to the crematory herself. "I was overwhelmed with a need to take care of this myself. It took away a sense of helplessness," she told me. Oddly enough, Carlson already knew she had the legal right to drive John to the crematory. About six months before John killed himself, Carlson had read an unpublished article by a fellow writer on how one would go about tending to one's own dead. It was legal in Vermont to deliver your loved one to the crematory or cemetery as long as it was done before the body started to decompose and all documents were in place, just as it was legal to bury your own on your property.

After getting prices from mortuaries ranging from $350 to

$850, Carlson saw a listing for the only crematory in the state—at Mount Pleasant Cemetery in St. Johnsbury, fifty miles away. Sure, the man there said, they'd take a body from a lay person. The charge $85. Carlson was sold.

Meanwhile, John's body was still in the truck and the police had called a local funeral director to bring it to the medical examiner's office for an autopsy. Carlson went outside to talk with him. It was this conversation in the chill of a snowy predawn, emotionally ensnarled in a surreal gloom from having just seen her dead husband slumped over in his truck, that planted a seed of bitterness for morticians in her mind. She questioned him about cremation charges: $60 for a cremation chipboard box; $50 to transport the body to the medical examiner's office and on to the funeral home, and a $350 service charge for the cremation itself. Carlson told the funeral director she'd found her own crematory, and just wanted him to bring John to the medical examiner and the funeral home, put him in a box, and wait for Carlson to pick him up. The funeral director was not pleased. "He just sneered at me," says Carlson, "and said, 'I'm in business to make money.'" The conversation ended here, and the funeral director went back to the authorities to wait for the word to load John into his vehicle and bring him to the medical examiner.

Carlson proceeded to call one of John's friends with a pickup truck. Sure, he'd be happy to help her out. When the town hall opened that morning she arranged with the town clerk to get a "burial transit permit." All that was left to do was pick up John's body and deliver him to St. Johnsbury. By 8:30 that night, Carlson and John's friend were plodding along in a snowstorm with John's chipboard box rattling in the back. It took about two hours to get there, and they were crying most of the way. When they arrived, Carlson opened the box for a final glimpse at John.

That spring, Carlson buried John's cremains in their garden.

SECOND HUSBAND, SECOND TRAGEDY

John's suicide moved Carlson, the writer, to launch a major project: She would write a book for others across the country who wanted to take the self-reliant route with their dead. She says she called 500 crematories and funeral directors, and by the time her research was done she had determined that in most states you could indeed take care of your own dead with no help from morticians, although some states require the funeral director to sign vital death documents and perform other functions, like the burial presence required in New York. A lot of work for naught, as Carlson couldn't find a publisher, and the project was put on hold.

In the meantime, Carlson had remarried. In 1986, tragedy struck her new husband, Steve Carlson. His mother had died of AIDS. Steve had three brothers and they all tended to their mother at home until the end. No outside help was needed. They got their documents, made her a pine box, dug her grave on a hill at an uncle's farm, and buried her there.

Steve's mother had encouraged Carlson to write more, and her death was the inspiration she needed to get this damned book published, one way or the other. In 1987 she and Steve published the book themselves. It sold modestly, a few national publications reviewed it, she did a few national talk shows and today is leader of the country's memorialites. Although it has only sold about 10,000 copies, it's become a staple of America's contemporary death-related literature.

TRICKS OF THE TRADE

Like other leading memorialites, Carlson's suspicion of the mortician constitutes a conspiratorial mind set. Complaints from fellow memorialites, who say they've been mistreated by morticians, and their private motives have created in them an enduring and what seems to be an eternal hostility toward the funeral industry. One of John Blake's often-repeated stories is of the funeral director who tells a client going for cremation, "Oh, so you want to burn your mother up?" There's no acknowledgement from the bashing-funeral director crowd that there might be a mortician or two out of about 80,000 or so across the country who might actually be compassionate human beings trying to provide whatever the customer wants. That in many small towns the funeral director is a community leader and friend whom a widow might invite over for a cup of coffee a few days after the funeral. The memorialites' condemnation is generally a blanket one: They're all bloody casket peddlers and embalming freaks; the system is wrong, all participants are guilty by association. This was the impression I got from dozens of conversations with dozens of memorialites. When I met some of them in Nashville at their 1996 conference, I came across a few who cut morticians some slack and were more concerned with getting more members in their organization and convincing them to plan for their funeral and cremation than condemning the Everyman funeral director.

Carlson says her goal as the new mother memorialite, as you might call her, is to let the media and the half-million elderly people who belong to the societies know what the morticians are really up to. In 1995 she produced a fifty-three-minute video for FAMSA called, *Understanding the Tricks of the Funeral Trade: Self Defense for Consumers.* It was paid for in part with a grant by FAMSA (yet a memorialite suspicious of getting ripped off by a mortician has to pay $29.95 plus shipping for the video.) The video box shows a smiling Carlson speaking to an audience of senior citizens. Plugging the video is none other than Jessica Mitford: "Lisa Carlson's presentation should be most useful," Mitford writes. "It explains much about what the consumer confronts in dealing with mortuaries and how to cope with fraudulent practices."

The tricks of the trade Carlson speaks of are nothing new. They're all manifestations of the most frequently heard criticism of the mortician: They exploit the emotional vulnerability of grieving survivors, who at this grim day of reckoning, "are a frazzled bundle of dendrites," as Carlson put it to me. It's the same thing critics have said again and again throughout the century. With consumer-beware defenses stifled from the shock of a loved one's death, they are ripe to be deceived and manipulated. It's a shameless enterprise indeed to profit off the dead. The funeral industry is indeed a dismal trade, and on and on. The difference today is, despite the crusades and government regulation, the merchandising keeps expanding and getting glitzier and more aggressive (see Chapter one), and death has become big business.

Carlson's gripes keep coming. "Embalming is not part of a traditional American funeral," she snapped when I suggested that many Americans consider embalming and a casket part of a traditional funeral and aren't ready to wash, cloth, box, and transport dead loved ones. "Traditional" Americans tended to their own dead, she points out, meaning premodern Americans.

Americans have been conned into accepting the American way of death. And our Funeral Rule doesn't help much, if any, because funeral directors routinely tell people embalming is required when it is not and don't give out price lists for caskets and vaults and general services like they're supposed to.

The trick that gets Carlson riled probably more than any other is when the mortician "steers people to expensive caskets." This is accomplished by keeping inexpensive caskets—like the cremation units discussed in Chapters one and two—in a shabby room away from the shiny metal and wood masterpieces laid out under mood lighting in a carpeted selection room. "It's fine to have a $10,000 gold-plated casket for those who want it, but you shouldn't hide the cheap caskets in the basement," says Carlson. "I had someone tell me they [the mortician] took them to a hall in the boiler room to look [at the cheap caskets]; I hear things like this all the time." This separation of expensive and cheap caskets, the Carlsonian reasoning goes, makes the casket shopper feel like a chump for being too cheap to spend a few extra dollars for one of these nice shiny caskets under the lights out in the nice room.

Another cheap casket trick Carlson will tell you about: selling them in one drab color, when fifteen or so colors are available. "These bastards," she told me, "never order it in any thing but gray!" Who wants to spend eternity in a gray casket, especially a cheap gray casket?

This kind of trickery isn't the exception, it's the rule, says Carlson. In the nine years since she published her book, she has heard, "bad experience after bad experience after bad experience, which makes it a little difficult not to get cynical." At the same time she faults people for becoming "willing victims. They know more about cars and toasters than death and dying." She recounts a comment from a young woman in the studio audience during one of her *Donahue* appearances "She said, 'Oh, I couldn't do that [tend to a dead loved one]. I fall apart when my cat dies.' We're a death-denying society, and funeral directors have perpetrated this with the formality of the funeral home."

Carlson believes there are far too many funeral homes out there and has data to prove it. In a blue information sheet she compiled for FAMSA—"Why the cost of dying may be much higher in your community"—she lists the total number of funeral homes, state-by-state, and the number that are needed. She figured how many are needed by concluding that on average one funeral home is needed for one death on a given day. She then took death statistics for each state and compared it with the number of mortuaries, without mentioning population fluctuations and other demographics within states that greatly affect why a certain number of funeral homes may be clustered in one area and dispersed in another. Anyhow, it's another conspiracy theory for the memorialites to ponder, and does point out the great number of mortuaries in states like New York, Pennsylvania, and Illinois. New York has about 1,900 funeral homes, more than any state; Carlson says just 666 are needed (a coincidence, she swears).

The problem with too many mortuaries is, of course, not enough death to go around. Many mortuaries do just 100 or less annual "cases" or "calls" (the industry words for bodies they handle). This means they've got to make as much on each call as they can. And this is why, Carlson rants, the nondeclinable basic service fee at so many mortuaries is $1,000 or more. It amounts to paying your funeral director a "waiting-around-until-you-die time fee. They want a full-time living from a part-time job."

After endless admonishments and condemnations, Carlson has room for some self-deprecating humor. She tells me that when Jessica Mitford was asked to describe who the memorialites of America are, she said, "Quakers, Unitarians, eggheads, and old farts."

ROOTIN' TOOTIN' TOTEN TUTORS

Karen Leonard keeps a few alternative containers in her garage, as in alternative to a casket, as in sturdy cardboard boxes people are cremated in, as in the nemesis of America's casketeers. She never knows when someone will call looking for help with a do-it-yourself death. If she runs out, she knows a mortuary that sells them for $148, still quite a mark-up from the wholesale price of about $30, but at least he sells them.

Leonard is executive director of the Redwood Funeral and Memorial Society in Sebastopol, California, and in recent years has emerged as the West Coast equivalent of Carlson (without the *Tricks* video). In 1996 Leonard began steering people who didn't want to work with a mortician or who couldn't afford one to a group of five women and a man who playfully call themselves, the Rootin' Tootin' Toten Tutors, with *Toten*, German for *death*, the operative word. The Tutors formed in December 1995 and in three months had handled two cases. They are an unusual blend of body transporter, document preparer, hospice worker, holistic healer, and compassionate friend. In April 1996 they were working with a gay couple, both with HIV, one dying from full blown AIDS, and were hoping to form a nonprofit group called the Natural Death Care Project, a place other than the mortuary to bring your dead, with no embalming, caskets or other traditional trappings.

The problem for Californians who want loved ones back when they die is that many hospital and crematory workers, morticians and public officials administering vital documents, don't realize that people legally responsible for the dead can bring them to the crematory or cemetery themselves. A corpse need not show up in a hearse or a funeral director's minivan. In some counties in California, the town clerk may refuse to release a death certificate to anyone but a funeral director, even though the next of kin or someone with durable power of attorney has the right, because that's the way it's always been done. If you're going the self-reliant route in Sonoma County, Leonard and the Tutors will direct you to Pleasant Hill Crematory, the only operation, they say, that will accept bodies from nonmorticians.

The Tutors take some pressure off Leonard, who has taken on a number of projects in recent years, most notably helping Jessica Mitford, who lived in Oakland, update *The American Way of Death*. Leonard has emerged as a kind of death industry consumer advocate à-la Ralph Nader. She's constantly trashing morticians for what she sees as the stranglehold they have on us, our death dollars, our right to tend to our dead. She began her career in the death industry in 1989 when she and a few friends opened Ghia Casket and Urn Outlet in San

Francisco, a death boutique selling handmade caskets, wearable urn jewelry, as seen in our tour of the Madelyn Booth at the NFDA convention, and other chic death paraphernalia, like an urn nine feet tall made of spiraled glass, and others that double as clocks. "If you're gonna put them on your shelf, put them to work, I say," quips Ghia salesman Tony Willoughby. Ghia doubles as art gallery/coffee house, with jazz bands and other entertainment.

Leonard says she quit Ghia after a few years when some elderly folk in Sonoma County asked her to form a memorial society to help them battle the local mortuaries who they said charged outrageous prices. In early 1996 she was railing at mortuaries charging as much as $1,500 for direct cremation and crematories that wouldn't accept bodies from nonmorticians in do-it-yourself cases. She courts the press and has been the subject of a handful of articles in which the local funeral directors come off as, as you'd expect, greedy opportunists. In March 1995 she was working with NBC's 20/20 news magazine on a funeral scam story "I have a victim with a blazing rip off story," she faxed me at the time. "She was sold the complete bill of goods . . . from embalming, solid copper casket, vault and above ground mausoleum. Alas, leaking vaults, exploded caskets and grisly results were the actual end product of all that money. Hardly 'peace of mind.' . . ."

Leonard reels off scores of death industry scams, like a memorial park sued for selling the same graves twice, a crematory charged for mass cremations, and for-profit cremation societies on the World Wide Web using the OGR suffix, which designates a nonprofit status.

She tells the story of an AIDS victim whose body was refused by a crematory in 1995 because it was brought there by a mortuary transit service, also called direct disposers or trade embalmers, depending on what part of the country you're in, or Leonard's preferred designation, direct disposition provider. These are people licensed to pick up and deliver bodies and not much else. To Leonard, they are another way to bypass the mortician. Leonard saved the AIDS victim $300 he didn't have by hiring the transporter. She says the California Cemetery Board (since disbanded) ordered the crematory not to accept the body after a local funeral director with clout complained about Leonard, who's gotten the local mortuary community a lot of bad press and is a general thorn in their side. Another crematory eventually handled the body after it spent a few weeks in limbo between the county morgue and the uncooperative crematory.

TO THE CREMATORY

Chris Sonnemann's father-in-law died one day in 1978 while working in his garden in Oakland, California. "He just keeled over and died," says Chris, now fifty years old and a pediatric hospice nurse who helps parents tend to their children after they've died. Her father-in-law was fifty-nine with a heart condition, but no one expecting he would die any time soon.

He was pronounced dead at the scene and taken to a funeral home. A funeral director called the family to say they would start embalming. No, thank you, the Sonnemanns responded, they had other plans. Here was another antimortician story with a trickle-down effect. "He disliked them," says Chris, speaking of funeral directors. "He felt he was ripped off when my mother-in law died. He thought they charged an outrageous price to transport her body from Wisconsin to Michigan. We knew he didn't want a conventional arrangement. He wanted his body cremated, so we told the funeral director we were coming to pick him up." The mortuary cooperated, and had the body waiting for them on a stretcher. The Sonnemanns wrapped him in a sheet and brought him to the crematory, where they purchased a corrugated cardboard box for $15.

This was the first time the crematory had a body delivered by lay people. About ten years later, a similar scenario was repeated with Sonnemann's father, with Chris assuming the traditional transport and wrapping chores of the mortician.

Today Chris works in Danville, California, just east of Oakland, helping children and teens die in their homes. And when they finally do, she helps parents bathe and clothe them, place them in a burial box or casket and drive them to the crematory or cemetery. Chris or a colleague secures the permit of disposition and death certificate and that's the end of it. No funeral director is involved.

In the past few years, Chris has handled a dozen cases. They've had a profound impact on the way she thinks about children and death. It's enough to say it's impossible to understand the soul-shaking catharsis a parent goes through when they are with their child to the very end: "The most horrifying thing a parent can do is to hand their child over to a stranger."

Often Chris uses her own vehicle to take the child to the mortuary or crematory: "The parents go with me and hold their child in the back seat. If we're going to the mortuary, someone meets us there with a gurney [a stretcher on rollers]. This is so much easier than handing [the child] over to someone else."

Chris remembers one couple in 1985 tending to their six-year-old son, who was dying of cancer at home. He died in the bed he was born in, and his parents decided to have a viewing at the house. Decomposition wasn't a factor because it was cool. The boy's father and uncle had built him a pine wood box, and friends and family scribbled messages and painted pictures on it. The boy was dressed in his "He Man" pajamas and visitors came to see him in his bed one last time. Then he was wrapped in a sheet, put in the pine box, carried to the car and taken to the crematory.

Chris tells another story of a fourteen-year-old girl she had known all her life who died recently at home of leukemia. Her father and brother carried her body out to their van, drove her to the mortuary, and carried the casket inside. "When I saw her mother the next day," remembers Chris, "it was the most awful-wonderful thing I had ever seen."

Unlike Leonard, Blake, Carlson, and the other pugnacious memorialites, Chris holds nothing personal against funeral directors, and can't be bothered with discussions of embalming, high cremation prices, and alternative containers. "My crusade is to make people aware of their options," she says. She even has a favorite funeral home, named, fittingly enough, Affordable Mortuary, in Walnut Creek. "They are wonderful, absolutely wonderful," she says, for one, because they've performed services for her children free of charge.

She likes to think that what she does transcends commerce. She is tending the crossroad of life and death for those whose life is being cut to just a glimpse by the cruel law of chance. "I feel I don't do this by myself," she says. "I feel the strength comes from some internal spiritual source. I realized a long time ago, I have no power over life and death. It comes from a higher source."

"DEATHING" THE REIKI MASTER

One of the Rootin' Tootin' Toten Tutors is Jerri Lyons, a teacher of the holistic hands-on-healing practice known as Reiki (pronounced Ray-kee). The Reiki practitioner, as Jerri describes it, channels the fundamental energy of the universe, subatomic particles if you will, to the client by touching them. Tending to the dead might not have been an outgrowth of Jerri's Reiki had not a Reiki master died. It was the death of this woman, Carolyn Whiting, Jerri's friend and mentor, that inspired her to delve into the arena of natural death.

Carolyn's main job was as an old-fashioned hospital nurse.

She took care of an elderly woman and taught Reiki on the side. Her students considered her spiritually advanced, and she was in great demand. She lived in Santa Rosa, in Sonoma County, and died unexpectedly in mid-1994 at the age of fifty-six. In her will were precise instructions for her postdeath ritual and the disposal of her body: No funeral directors, no embalming, no casket. Friends were to take care of everything.

A few of her closest friends read the will and heeded Carolyn's call. The first order of business was getting the Petaluma Valley Hospital to turn Caroline's body over to them. The people in charge had apparently never had a request for a body from lay people, and it took a day before paper work was secured and the authorities released Carolyn to them—in a body bag. They lugged her out to their van and drove to Carolyn's home.

Friends were waiting there, including Jerri, who had laid out a futon for the body and found a nice dress in Carolyn's closet to dress her in. Jerri had seen a few dead bodies before, including her parents at traditional wakes, and a friend, Cindy, laid out at her home in Seattle in 1984: "She looked like a skeleton." Jerri hadn't thought much about being around dead people and wondered if Carolyn might look as bad as Cindy. "We saw Carolyn all the time, and she was very alive, a very vibrant person. She did a lot of healing with a lot of people and had a great sense of humor. She was always laughing a lot. This is how we remembered her. We didn't know what her coloring would be like. It was very odd to have her in a body bag. That was strange."

Carolyn was carried into the house, and the body bag was laid on the futon. "When we took her out of the body bag," Jerri remembers, "we were in shock. She looked so beautiful, like she could open her eyes and say hi to us. Her coloring was fairly normal, although she was a bit pale and cold, for sure—she'd been in the morgue—and a bit stiff, and that's why we decided to cut her clothes off. After that we washed her body—four women, all washing her body. I felt like we were midwives for the dead. I felt like we were preparing her for the next world, like we were birthing her into the next world, some would say deathing her into the next world. There was a lot of love in the handling of her body.

"Touching her body was making it very real for us. We also spoke to her, and we were giving her Reiki. We spoke to her body, and when we had a problem getting her rings off, Patty [Hiller, a friend] talked to her and said, 'Carolyn, would you help us get the rings off.' I know rigor mortis sets in, but it's temporary from what I found out later, and it felt as though she really did relax, and we got the rings off. I had never felt that emotional around death. We kept getting messages from her. We had great waves of grief and great waves of joy. It all felt very much orchestrated by her [Carolyn], the way things came together synchronistically."

Jerri had found "a really beautiful turquoise dress, with gold embroidering" and they put it on Carolyn. Jerri applied a little makeup—"someone said she'd never leave the house without makeup"—Carolyn's feet were left bare, and it was time for the ceremony to begin.

Carolyn was moved to the living room. By this time about twelve people were in the house. "We chanted, read poetry, we cried," remembers Jerri. "At one point someone said, 'Show me a sign that you're not gonna come back around' [that she was definitely dead]. And her cat walked right across her like she wasn't even there. At that point Norma [Wilcox, Carolyn's best friend] knew." A couple of psychics were present, and they did some "channeling" with Carolyn. "These are people who communicate with people who have crossed over. Some people have a hard time adjusting to being on the other side, Carolyn was fine."

The ceremony wound down. Everyone left except Norma

and Patty who kept vigil over Carolyn's body through the night. In the morning, Jerri and a few others came back to prepare her for the crematory. Some final touches had been added. Someone got the idea to tape fortune cookie fortunes Carolyn collected on her body. A wing of a small bird she kept at home was affixed to her chest, a piece of driftwood placed snugly in her hand. And on her belly button was taped a "tachyon energy cell, a healing tool, a little stained glass bubble," as Jerri describes it. "Carolyn was communicating with us about what she would like to die with. It was like Carolyn to be light about this. Death doesn't have to be awful and depressing."

Adorned for the crematory, Carolyn's friends carried her on the futon to the van and loaded her inside. The crematory operator had a box waiting, and Carolyn was lifted out of the van.

That night the cremains were returned in a plastic bag, itself in a cardboard box. "We did Reiki to the bag, they were a vessel for her energy," says Jerri. "Then we took the ashes out and put them into tiny bags so we could scatter them around the world. I took three baggies and brought one of them on a rafting trip to Northern California. And I said to my friends, 'I brought these ashes of my friend, Carolyn, and I'm going to scatter them in the water.' And I released them, and there was a little left in the bag, and I reached over the side of the raft to wash out the baggie, and this huge dragon fly landed on the baggie. And I said, 'Look everybody.' And one guy said, 'Looks like her spirit has really materialized.' She knew I was honoring her, and the dragon fly was the sign."

Carolyn's death convinced Jerri she should intensify her Reiki as well as make a contribution to the natural death movement. "Carolyn has worked with me from the other side. She's working through me. I felt like a sister to her."

The Carolyn incident led to collaboration with the Rootin' Tootin' Toten Tutors, which Jerri reminds me is a very serious project, and the alliterative name will probably be dropped. In late March when I talked to her she and a few Tutors had met with the gay couple and told them they were there to help them plan their deaths. The man who was dying faded in and out of consciousness, probably from morphine, and Jerri proceeded to administer a dose of hands-on-healing. The couple wasn't sure how they wanted to handle their deaths, but the Tutors would be there when they decided.

"The focus is to help people do self-directed disposition, becoming your own funeral director," Jerri explains. "People are very emotional when this happens, and it's hard for them to fill out paperwork. These are the kinds of things we can do for them, but the main thing we do is support them as part of a community of friends. We believe that by participating it helps with grieving and a healing experience comes with that. People's hearts are very much open at this time, and there's so much appreciation for us. All barriers of fear and anger are broken down, and there's a lot of room for love."

Jerri's fellow Tutor, forty-nine-year-old Mary Olsen, also decided to help the living tend to their dead after taking care of her best friend, a victim of pancreatic cancer. It was a kind of religious experience for Mary: "It made me realize there's a thin veil between the physical and spiritual, and it's thinnest between birth and death. It's all one spiritual thing, and you come in, and you go out, like a loop."

Mary is the mainstream Tutor; no hands-on-healing, no spiritual channeling. She was a manager at Safeway for ten years and recently an assistant to a marriage and family counselor. She takes care of the business side of things, like setting up the project as a nonprofit educational group. Their work is no less than an attempt to "transform the culture in the area of death." Her criticism of the funeral industry isn't personal, it's the nature of the beast: "They [morticians] may be very nice, but they're all expensive and they're all about making money, big-time."

BEATING THE MORTICIAN ON MARTHA'S VINEYARD

Carol Buhrman died at her daughter's home on Martha's Vineyard in October 1993. She was sixty-one years old. Colon cancer. The hospice nurse had been there to administer morphine throughout her final days.

The hospice nurse was there the day Carol died. When she saw the homemade coffin in the bedroom, she seemed alarmed and was silent. She left and some time later called Carol's daughter, Jan Buhrman, to tell her that what she and her husband were planning to do—bury Carol themselves with no help from the funeral director—was illegal. The nurse said she had checked on this with a leading Boston mortician who sat on the state funeral regulatory board.

The Buhrmans are self-reliant types. "We're pretty much naturalists," says Jan, pointing out that her mother died at home, she gave birth at home, and her husband, a carpenter, built their house from scratch. He also built Carol's coffin after pricing caskets at the local mortuary and finding the cheapest, a particle board box, sold for $875.

Carol's death was simple, the way the Buhrmans wanted it. It was bad enough to have to deal with the acute sadness of losing your mother. Now Jan had to deal with intrusive and money-hungry morticians.

Jan had made arrangements with the local cemetery. She bought a plot for $200 and a grave liner (concrete box) for $400. The gravedigger would get $200, a stonecutter $99, for carving Carol's name in an uncut stone. A Scottish bagpiper charged $100 for blowing Celtic spirits in honor of Carol's Irish roots. And finally, the minister would get a $50 honorarium. It cost them $100 for materials for the coffin.

Now the Buhrmans were being told the local funeral director was required by law to view the body and transport it to the cemetery. The price: $1,900. Jan heard them correctly. She called the Boston mortician the hospice nurse had called, and sure enough, he repeated what he had told the nurse, and said if Jan didn't have the $1,900 he could refer her to a welfare agency that would provide an alternative arrangement. "He told me absolutely I could not bury my own mother," remembers Jan.

The Buhrmans weren't buying the morticians' line and proceeded with their plan. "If they had a problem with not viewing the body," Jan told me, "they could dig it up."

At 10 A.M., the morning after Carol died, twenty friends and family gathered at the Buhrmans and headed out to the cemetery. Carol was in her coffin in a pickup truck. Some how the minister had gotten the death certificate from the funeral home. This allowed the cemetery to issue a burial permit. Jan remembers: "The gravedigger and cemetery caretaker told us nobody had ever done this before, and it was kind of nice to see somebody beat the system."

Four days after the burial, the minister called Jan: She had to go down to the funeral home to sign a release form. When she got there the funeral director said if she didn't sign the form he'd lose his license, because he had signed the death certificate without seeing the body. He also wanted $500 for his trouble. Jan couldn't believe what she was hearing. She wrote him a check for $100 and walked out the door.

Not long after this ordeal Jan became a memorialite at the Boston Memorial Society.

MUMMY RENAISSANCE

He calls himself Corky Ra, and he says he has 140 people he's going to transform into authentic mummies, à-la King Tut. They'll be dead of course, and Corky's mummy company is to be paid out of special life insurance policy covering mummification. (From $32,000 to more than $150,000 for gold and other pricey "Mummiforms.") Call it Pharaoh's Preneed.

Corky says he's already mummified a few dozen animals that were subsequently entombed in mausolea and private residences. "We just finished two dogs for a National Geographic program," he told me in April 1996.

You may have heard about Corky's company, Summum, which received a rash of national media exposure in the late 1980s and early 1990s, including a treatment on the talk show circuit. It was another one of those kooky American fads. In recent years, Corky has jumped on the health and fitness bandwagon by merging aerobics to Summum's meditation/self-help philosophy. When not in the animal embalming lab, Corky might be found in workout gear leading Summumites in something called Forever Fit Aerobics.

Summing up Summum's mummy service: "Memorialization through Permanent Body Preservation." This is a line from Summum sales literature. Unlike the temporary American fix of embalming-casket-vault, mummies are forever.

As of mid-1996, Corky, whose real name is Claude Nowell, was still waiting for one of his mummies-to-be to die, although, like the funeral director and cemeterian with pay-before-you-die policy holders, it's not spoken of in such insensitive terms. Summum applicants are forty to sixty years old, and there's more than a few movie stars and assorted celebrity types signed up, says Corky, which is his childhood nickname.

Tabloids had a field day with Summum: "Mummy Dearest," declared an April 1992 headline of the *Sun*. "Now your relatives can turn you into the poor man's King Tut." *XS* magazine detailed the strange death desires of a handful of Corky's clients in an article in August 1991 that carried the headline, "Mummy's The Word . . . Turn Your Mummy into a Mummy." Kay Henry, a former radio talk show host, said she would spend $50,000 to be mummified with her microphone, TV, CD player, and stuffed animals wrapped up with her body. Body-conscious

Janet Greco, of Salt Lake City, thirty-eight years old at the time, told XS she wanted to be mummified because she worked out a lot and ate right. "It doesn't make sense to spend all this time taking care of my body and then discard it," she told XS.

YOU FIGURE IT OUT

The story of Summum starts with some kind of revelation Corky says he experienced in the fall of 1975 in his native Salt Lake City. Whatever it was inspired him to found a new philosophy he called Summum Bonum Amen Ra, which he says is ancient Egyptian for, "Sum Total Worker on Creation." Corky wrote a book laying out this philosophy—"a reconciliation of all philosophies and religions into one," he tells me, within the context of ancient Egyptian practices and death rituals. It's essentially a self-help pseudo philosophy leaning heavily on meditation and Corky's unusually unclear personal vision.

As bizarre as it may sound, the cornerstone of Summum was making wine—"sacramental wines" Corky calls Summum Nectar Publications. He made and makes this wine in a pyramid-shaped building he built in Salt Lake City. The pyramid provided the right vibe for the creation of the wine, supposedly modeled after the original stuff used by the Egyptians. The wine would be used with meditation in Summum's "program of Mindfulness and in the process of Mummification," according to Corky.

Corky says he's taught Summum to thousands of people and that he exports his wine around the world.

By 1980 he had legally changed his name to Summum Bonum Amen Ra. Corky was now Summum, and today he's referred to in newspaper articles as Mr. Ra. He had been thinking of making mummies as early as 1976 when people would visit his wine-making pyramid and ask, "Where are the mum-

mies?" He also says his mortician friends and a pathologist pal
made him consider branching out from wine and meditation.
These friends told Corky that the "unspoken joke" of the funeral industry was the fact that people were led to believe their
bodies were being preserved with embalming and caskets and
vaults, as discussed in previous chapters. "People were paying
$5,000 for a casket. I said, 'You've got to be kidding me.' Why
do they buy the casket? Why not just buy a vault and let the
body decompose? I thought, why not provide something that
will give people what they think they've been getting."

Corky and his team of mummy makers proceeded to patent
special embalming techniques for his mummification process.
He says they mummified thirty people who were donated to a
medical school and eventually cremated; that's why they are no
where to be found today. At the same time Corky started mummifying animals.

In 1985 Corky decided to exhibit at the NFDA convention,
like the one detailed in Chapter one, to show off his new mummification embalming patents. That year the convention was at
Caesar's Palace in Las Vegas. At the booth next to Corky's was
a Florida embalming teacher-cum-mummifier, a man named
John Chew.

The rest is history. Corky would concentrate on animals in
Salt Lake City (as well as teaching Forever Fit Aerobics and
selling wine) and Chew would handle humans at Lynn
University in Boca Raton, Florida, where he ran the mortuary
school program. Corky had found a partner.

Chew's been to Egypt and back a few times since—he's an
avid Egyptologist and amateur archaeologist—and he's still
waiting for his first body to mummify. Hopes were high in 1993
that a Summum candidate would finally cross over, but, alas,
nature turned a different course. The person in question had
terminal cancer, but it went into remission. Corky points out to
me that Summum "is not really waiting for anyone to die.
We're promoting an option in the funeral industry. I don't see

any of our clients dying any time soon. As a matter of fact, I might be the first to go." Corky is fifty-three years old.

Chew can be seen standing next to various "Mummiforms" —the actual sarchopagus mummy case into which the body to be mummified is sealed up—in a dozen or so newspaper and magazine articles on Summum. In November 1992, he gave a succinct description in the *Boca Raton Monday Paper* of what he'll be doing as soon as a Summumite dies: "We'll soak the body with salts and highly sophisticated chemicals, wrap it in 100 to 500 yards of gauze and fancy lines, coat it with polyurethene, seal it in a mummiform, and weld it shut." Left out is the procedure of removing lungs and intestines, placing them in liquid preservatives and returning them to their original location; as well as removing the brain, and making a "death mask" for the sarcophagus, crafted by an artist from an imprint of the dead person's face.

TIMOTHY LEARY'S DEAD

On his Beverly Hills death bed, seventy-five-year-old LSD guru Timothy Leary was sucking nitrous oxide from balloons to ease the pain of the cancer that would soon consume him. "He said to me, 'This is my last balloon,' and he looked me right in the eye, and I knew that that was it." This is the word from Leary's friend and deathbed companion, Carol Rosin, one of the "evolutionary agents," in the "genetic hall of fame," in Leary's book, *The Intelligence Agents*. "He was now going to release himself out of his body, and he laid down on that bed and started this slow process of breathing." At 12:44 A.M., May 31, 1996, Timothy Leary was indeed dead, and Rosin remembers, "I got a huge rush of warmth that burst through my body. It really startled me." One of America's most eccentric 1960s counter-culture figures was now history, at least on the physical plane, and Rosin set about the task of preparing for a journey where few men had gone before.

"He said he wanted to be cremated and he also wanted to go out into space, and he wanted me to get him there. And I promised I would get him into space," said Rosin. Who else to call but NASA, which told Rosin about a new company based in Houston called Celestis, which for $4,800 will pack a few grams of your cremains into a little titanium container (the size of lipstick) and launch it on a commercial rocket carrying satellite payloads into space. Leary was sold after he watched the Celestis promotional video a few days before he died. And so a pinch of Timothy Leary's cremains, along with those of Star Trek creator Gene Roddenberry and another twenty or thirty mortals, were to have been blasted into space in the fall of 1996 aboard a three-stage rocket dropped from the belly of a modified L-1011 jet plane at 50,000 feet over the Canary Islands. A year to ten years after the rocket reached orbit, it would fizzle, and Leary and the others would re-enter the atmosphere in a spectacular burnout.

"This is not a space burial," said Celestis spokesman Gary Gartner, a former NASA official who formed the company with other NASA scientists in 1995. "This is a postcremation memorial service. We have ten funeral homes in California marketing our service and we feel this is a global market." Celestis plans four launches a year; most of them will be ground launches, opposed to Leary's 50,000-foot liftoff. The $4,800 covers a spot at the launch site for survivors: "Have you ever seen a rocket launch?" says Gartner. "It is really a special occasion. Survivors will come to the launch and it will be one of the most thrilling experiences in their life."

Leary told Rosin he expected to be connecting with the eternal light somewhere in the cosmos, and when his rocket burns out, probably some time in the early twenty-first century, he'll be making his final splash in the physical world: "We were talking about his dying," says Rosin, "and he thought this experience of going into space would be awesome. He said, 'Surely I'm going to be famous for this one. I'll be visible and seen for and miles and miles around.'"

8

WHAT'S GOOD
FOR PAPA JOHN

The funeral is not the casket, and the casket is not the funeral, just part of it.

—Howard Raether, veteran funeral association official.

What was good for Papa John when he died in 1990 was an embalming, a gray pin-striped suit, and a rental casket. At the time his wife didn't think so; she wanted him cremated without ceremony and scattered on the farm. No funeral, no viewing. Just get it over with. But Papa John's friends, the husband–wife funeral directors, knew the family needed closure.

Papa John Walkup was a chemistry professor and tobacco farmer in Danville, Kentucky, population 14,000. By the time he died, he was in his eighties, had suffered several strokes, and had trouble walking. Mrs. Walkup and her son, Johnny, a cattleman who lived next door with his wife and two daughters, knew Papa John was on his way out. He died at home on the farm one evening in March. Johnny summoned his best friend, Robert Hamlin, and his wife, Mary Hamlin, both funeral directors.

When the Hamlins arrived, Papa John was in his bedroom. It was eight o'clock. They joined the Walkups at a kitchen table where they sipped coffee and sodas and talked about Papa John's long illness. A decision needed to be made, and Mrs. Walkup, "a tiny, sweet little old lady, five feet tall, 100 pounds," according to Mary, had made it: Papa John would be cremated right away, and she'd scatter his cremains somewhere on the land. Mrs. Walkup was, according to Mary, a reserved woman, uncomfortable with the thought of people mingling around her husband's body at a viewing. Papa was a salty old codger, "an ornery old cuss," in the words of Mary, but he'd lived in town for years and had many friends who would no doubt show up to view him one last time. Mrs. Walkup had no problem with a bodiless memorial service, but the thought of Papa John embalmed and laid out in a casket—perish the thought! Seeing the dead body is supposed to help people reach closure, according to grief and bereavement experts, and the Hamlins will tell you from their encounters with the bereaved that this is indeed the case. But Mrs. Walkup wasn't buying. "She was in denial," Robert says. "She thought if she didn't have to go through the funeral service she could go back to her routine."

What about Johnny's wife and his two teenage daughters, who were vacationing on the shore of North Carolina? The Hamlins were convinced they would want to see Papa John before he disappeared forever. "He was like a second father to the girls," Mary told me. "And if they came home from the beach and he was gone and cremated, he would just disappear from their lives, and that might not be good for them. I told Mrs. Walkup we shouldn't do anything unchangeable until they got back." Another words: Let's hold off on the cremation until we think this through. In the meantime, Robert and Johnny excused themselves for a tête-à-tête at Johnny's place.

"Johnny told Robert he wanted Papa John embalmed for a viewing," said Mary, "and they figured Mrs. Walkup would eventually agree. Robert told Johnny we had a rental casket, or he could come in and see Papa John on the gurney [a stretcher-like contraption]. Johnny went for the rental casket."

When the men returned, Mrs. Walkup, still convinced her granddaughters would have no desire to see their dead grandpa in a casket, reluctantly agreed: Go ahead and embalm Papa John, if that's what everyone wants. Mrs. Walkup would get her cremation, and the grandchildren would get their viewing.

It was midnight before all this was settled. Papa John would need a suit, a nice burial suit for the final viewing. Robert asked Mrs. Walkup where he might find one. She didn't know. It had been so long since he was out and about. It was clear her heart wasn't in this whole embalming-viewing strategy, so Robert decided he'd get Papa John a burial suit at the funeral home.

The next day Papa John was embalmed, shaved, rouged, dressed in a pin-striped suit, and put in a rental casket. He'd let himself go toward the end and hadn't looked this good in a long time, the Hamlins say. "He was clean," explains Mary. "It was the difference between someone with a shaggy haircut and a trim. You know how much better someone looks when they're neat and clean? And the embalming puts fluid back into the skin, so it takes on a better appearance. The fluid diffuses out to all the tissues and skin looks much better." The suit, selling for $100, and casket, renting for $485, were on the house. The plan was for a private viewing for family only (an option given to the brother and sister in the cremation casket video in Chapter two), followed by an open visitation to the public with closed casket.

Mrs. Walkup was still unenthused about the viewing and encouraged her granddaughters to bypass Papa John's viewing. "She got a hold of 'em and said, 'Y'all don't want to see him,'" remembers Mary. "And the girls agreed." But the girls' mother overruled Mrs. Walkup and in they went to take a final look.

Meanwhile, "Mrs. Walkup sat out in the hall and refused to look in at Papa John," says Mary, "and the girls came out and pleaded with her to come see him. `Grandma, you need to come see him, he looks so good. Grandma, he looks so much better.' She never did go in to see him." The Hamlins were proud of their re-creation of Papa John.

For the granddaughters, Mary says this must have been some kind of a catharsis: "This brought back to them all the memories of what a wonderful person he was. He was looking better than what they remembered when he was alive, and they saw that death was better than what he was going through alive."

Johnny and his family said their goodbyes to Papa John before the casket was closed and the public was let in for a viewing. When everyone had left, Papa John was loaded into a van and driven to a crematory in Lexington, fifty miles away. The next day, about 100 people turned out for a service at Danville's Presbyterian Church. A month later, Mrs. Walkup came by the funeral home to pick up Papa John's cremains.

I met Robert Hamlin, a portly man of forty-eight with thin brown hair combed neatly over a shiny forehead, in February 1996 in Lexington, at the Kentucky Funeral Directors Association Mid-winter Conference. I had just finished giving a speech when Robert came up to me in the hotel lobby, where a few hundred morticians in suits mingled between programs. It was like I was back at the NFDA convention.

Robert was interested in a company in California I had talked about that arranges funerals so survivors conduct them, a progressive idea tapping an untraditional spirit toward funeral and burial that has always surfaced—this century—in California. Robert himself didn't perform by the book. He made house calls for nearly all his clients, just like the casketeering undertakers of the nineteenth century. That's what modern funeral directing was all about, Robert was telling me, giving people want they want: "If we don't give people service, they're not gonna need us any more."

By the time the conversation turned to cremation, which I spent quite a bit of time on in my speech, Robert was pointing a finger into my tie to drive home a point: "Funeral directors have got to get their heads out of their asses and get their cremation prices up there." The cremation factor in Kentucky was tradition. Cremation was all but unheard of twenty-five years ago. And with just a 5.3 percent cremation rate—2,000 cremations per 38,000 deaths—Kentucky cremates less of its dead than all but three or four other states. But when you're used to a lifetime of funeral and burial in a land of God-fearing traditionalists, a cremation comes along and the funeral director is apt to turn it over to someone else or do a bare minimum direct cremation. For Robert, cremation could be handled with a rental casket, like Papa Johns. The only thing different than the old days is that the body goes to the crematory rather than the cemetery.

It was during this conversation that Robert told me about Papa John. A month later I called the Hamlins to flesh out the details. As the saga of Papa John concluded, we moved on to other areas.

"This is about a 200-call town," says Robert, meaning about 200 people die in Danville each year. These 200 bodies are divvied up between three mortuaries, Stith Funeral Home, where the Hamlins work, a firm which handles most of the black calls, and another mortuary. Robert says his edge is making house calls, just like the old-time country doctor, or a cemetery grave prospector, for that matter. Sitting at the kitchen table with Mrs. Walkup and Johnny wasn't the exception. Experience has taught Robert that people want to make decisions about embalming and burial and funerals and viewing in the comfort of their home. Robert's out to make a profit, just as any business man, and the way he does it is by taking care of families. This doesn't mean he gives anything away, notwithstanding Papa John's suit and rental casket. In a 200-call town, you'd best make each call profitable. This explains Robert's concern about getting those cremation prices up there.

It's the little touches that count. "I've taken donuts to a family at 6:30 in the morning," he says, "and we'll sit around the kitchen table and just talk. We take families a home register book, and give 'em little stickers to put on dishes to write the names of people on, so they don't have to worry about who the dishes belong to when they return them." And sometimes, if it's a friend, or a friend of a friend, which is likely in this 200-call town, Robert will sit with the grieving survivors, like the wife of a friend who died in March 1996, and they'll have "a good cry together."

One of the funeral industry's legendary leaders, Howard Raether, NFDA executive director for decades, once said something you hear from old-timer funeral directors unhappy with the industry's casket mania: "The funeral is not the casket, and the casket is not the funeral, just part of it." Robert's version goes: "Any body can sell a casket, Sears Roebuck can sell a casket. But nobody can take care of a family like I can."

9

The Memorialites Go to Nashville

T he memorialites have chosen
a great time to come to Nashville for their biennial conference.
It's the end of May 1996 and the days are warm, sunny and
breezy. The weather is matched by the beautiful location
they've chosen. They've not done as the funeral directors did
eighteen months ago for their 1994 expo. They are not at
Nashville's convention center of choice, Opryland, the indoor
tropical rain forest-cum-glossy mall-cum-Grand Ole Opry,
where I met Mrs. Tommy Austin, burial gown maker, and the
other funeral show characters. Not only is Opryland expensive,
it's also not the right environment for a group of about 125
Unitarians, Quakers, professional mortician bashers, consumer
activists, social workers, and a smattering of other interested
elderly parties who band together every two years for fellowship
and to chart new strategies in their crusade not to pay a lot for
the final transaction of their lives and the lives of their peers
and to have a few laughs over the absurdities of the business of
death. This year some of the laughs will come from a viewing

of the BBC documentary, *Over My Dead Body,* which trashes America's death industry and had about twenty-five memorialites in hysterics one evening during the conference. Their day of reckoning may be coming, but it seems they figure there's no sense taking it too seriously.

The memorialites are meeting under their umbrella group of 140 societies, the Funeral and Memorial Societies of America (FAMSA), the offspring of the first cremation cooperative founded in Seattle nearly sixty years ago. They are ten miles from Opryland at the Scarritt-Bennett Retreat and Conference Center, a converted theological college run by the United Methodist Women. They are paying $48 a night for a tidy little dormitory room and three square meals at a dining hall. It's a ten-acre campus dominated with buildings made of native Tennessean stone, built in the 1920s when Kansas City's Scarritt school for missionaries relocated to Nashville. (By 1988, the United Methodist Women took over and turned it into a center and retreat for nonprofit groups and a place where missionaries come for reunions.) The buildings form a quad of sweeping trees—crimson maple, Bradford pear, dogwood, magnolia—and there's a little organic garden adjoining a very green lawn intersected with concrete paths lit with black Dicksenian street lamps, great for a stroll to savor the sweet early summer days. It's a quiet, contemplative place; you can imagine monks in brown cloaks and hoods moving softly across the lawn to the chapel for evening vespers. A Gothic tower rises up like a cathedral and adjoins a dining hall with rows of original wood tables that seat about thirty (and are protected from beverage rings by a cashier who reminds you how old and well preserved they are, so please keep your beverages on your tray). The memorialites lounge in the administration building's parlor and living room, graced with highly polished antique furniture on Persian rugs over rustic wood floors.

Accommodations are spartan by standards of most American business and educational conferences. No phones or televisions in the dorms. Forget about room service or even getting a drink—the Scarritt-Bennett campus is dry, the strongest beverage you'll find here is coffee. Most everyone shares a bathroom, although I have my own, no doubt an amenity for one of just a few nonmemorialites at the conference. My bed is a cozy twin and a sign on the wall asks me to please put my linen out in the hall when I leave. At my last funeral show at the Peabody Hotel in Orlando, my company paid nearly $200 a night for a ritzy room with a TV in the bathroom.

As you'd expect, they'll be no trade show here. The memorialites, national guardians of a half a million of our elderly's right not to spend a small fortune on their death, are the last people you'll see displaying glossy caskets, hearses, and models laid out on embalming tables. The casket is as maligned here as cigarettes would be at a gathering of the American Lung Association. But as I enter the lobby of the auditorium where the memorialites are meeting, I see a couple of cremation boxes, the alternative containers the federal government requires funeral homes to make available to shoppers who say thanks but no thanks to caskets. It turns out one death industry supplier is here—none other than Elder Davis, the cremation casket specialist with the zealous marketing campaign of newsletters and consultants, where you'll read and hear language like "satisfying cremation consumers," and direct cremation being "the great insult to death care." It's a strange juxtaposition, this minidisplay from Elder Davis. They are one of industry's hot new kids on the block and have grabbed a healthy chunk of the cremation dollar with their lookalike fake caskets and no-nonsense corrugated fiberboard cremation boxes. And here they are at the meeting of a group that for years has spread the word about the trappings of death products and services. Yet the memorialites seem to have found a friend in Elder Davis. It may be part of the death industry, but it makes cremation containers you can buy for as little as $100, the kind you'll find in the garage of Karen Leonard, the mortician-attacking memorialite in Sonoma County, California, whom I'll soon be meeting.

The containers were brought here by two Elder Davis employees who loaded them into their station wagon at company headquarters in Richmond, Indiana, and hit the road for Nashville. They're here at the request of Lisa Carlson, author of *Caring For Your Own Dead*, who will be named FAMSA's new executive director at this conference. Any doubts I may have had about Carlson's extreme antimortician sentiments quickly dissipated after seeing her in action. I had talked to her several times a few months earlier (see Chapter seven) and knew she was a leading nemesis of the death industry. Now I heard her issue a "call to social action" to fellow memorialites. It would be a holy war of sorts, this fight against the Everyman mortician, and the memorialites had no one but themselves to wage the battle. They needed to be ever vigilant to protect the public against the "extortionist"—a word Carlson seems to use every few minutes when she's addressing an audience—prices of the funeral industry. They needed to fight funeral directors on state regulatory boards protecting rules forbidding the sale of caskets anywhere but at mortuaries. They needed to protect preneed dollars. Break up the "cozy relations" between the National Funeral Directors Association and the Federal Trade Commission, who Carlson says are colluding to allow mortuaries to charge "extortionist" basic service fees, which is why you'll find direct cremations going for as much as $1,500. A favorite rant of Carlson's is that "there are too many funeral homes that want full-time pay for part-time work," referring to the hundreds, if not a few thousand mortuaries that handle maybe fifty or fewer funerals a year, and so, the argument goes, they must charge those "extortionist" prices to survive.

As they battle the forces protecting a system that allows shameless dollars to be made off dead bodies, the memorialites will attract new members and the media. "When you become a group of social action," Carlson said during one of her conference talks, "you suddenly open membership to everyone. Because

who is against consumers' rights? It appeals to everyone."
Including the media, ever ready to expose wrongdoing in the
name of consumer ripoffs, and thus "... aren't as likely to write
about cheap funerals as they are about social action," says
Carlson, who knows this first hand, as she and Karen Leonard
are often quoted in local and national newspaper and magazine
articles on death industry scandals and consumer-beware
reports.

Lest any memorialite think the status quo of negotiating
cheap prices with reasonable morticians and increasing membership was enough, Carlson had a message:

*"And I guess I would ask you why we exist at all. If the
funeral options available to everyone were perfect, why
would we have a reason to be existing? If every funeral
director, every mortuary in the country offered fair prices,
a wide range of options, did not indulge in manipulating
the public, did not hide the cheap caskets, did not domi-
nate the funeral board with self-serving regulations, did
not limit the options for caring for your own dead in certain states, did not say that only funeral directors can sell
caskets in North Carolina, there would be no reason for
our existence. And so I am saying there is a huge reason
for our existence, both at the national organization and
at on a local level."*

And one final thing Carlson had to say. Jessica Mitford
was updating her best-seller, *The American Way of Death*, and
she hadn't yet decided how to portray today's memorialites.
Carlson suggested to the audience that how "Decca," Mitford's
nickname, treats them in her book depends on whether she got
a good report back from this conference from Karen Leonard,
Decca's research assistant: "Decca refers to memorial society
members as Unitarians, Quakers, eggheads, and old farts,"
Carlson explains, in another of her familiar lines. "I guess I

should ask, do we want to leave that image for Jessica, or do we want to do something about it?"

Midford died about seven weeks later.

BASTARDS . . . RASCALS

A few months before I met her, Carlson had told me on the phone that funeral directors were "bastards" for only offering alternative containers in one color, usually a drab gray, when many nice colors are available. And now here, as we sat on a bench in the quad with a warm breeze sweeping across us, her cigarette snuffed out, her throat cleared with a few raspy coughs, Carlson, a short and stocky middle-aged woman wearing black slacks and a blue blouse, with short black hair cropped in bangs, put the alternative container issue this way: "The cloth-covered, particle, crepe-lined casket comes in fifteen colors, and as a rule the only color they [funeral directors] order it in gray, and I've got one rascal who keeps it on display with a torn lining, because in Vermont they are required to have at least one model of their low-end casket on display. But if a priest dies they order it in burgundy or some other color." It seems Carlson wants a body in an alternative container as much as casketeers want them in caskets. The same goes for her sidekick, Karen Leonard, who flew in for the conference with Jerri Lyons, one of the Rootin' Tootin' Totum Tutors, the hands-on-healing death walker/mortician alternative, as she might be called. Leonard will be introducing the memorialites to some sites on the World Wide Web at an evening session, including the "Funeral and Ripoffs" site of Fr. Henry Wasielewski, a retired Roman Catholic priest holed up with his computer in Tempe, Arizona, pumping out volumes of scathing indictments against funeral directors (thirty pages as of mid-1996), including what he says is a "top-secret" list of casket wholesale prices exposing the—here's that word again—"extortionist" conspiracy leveled against the American public by these scheming undertakers.

WHITE CREMATION BOXES

Suzy O'Donnell is one of the two Elder Davis reps here, a C*O*P*E (*Cremation Oriented Product Engineered*) coordinator, as she calls herself. She met Carlson at a funeral show in California, and Carlson invited her to bring a couple of white prototype alternative containers to the conference. The idea was to have containers that survivors could draw, paint, and write on for farewell messages before the body was taken to the crematory. Carlson had received a request for such containers from some hospice people she works with.

Kids with crayons would have a field day on these two bright rectangular boxes. One is as simple as you get: A long white box made of "triple wall" corrugated fiberboard, a little harder than a UPS box, that will hold anyone under seven-feet tall and, my guess, under 300 pounds. There's a flat white lining but no pillow, fluffy mattress, or decorations. Elder Davis calls it, appropriately enough, the White Corrugated Container Prototype. It leans against the wall outside the auditorium in two easy pieces, the lid and the box itself, and sells wholesale for $50 and for perhaps $100 to $200 at the mortuary. The second box, laid out on a table, is the granddaddy of alternative containers, the elite First Step, discussed in a previous chapter. It's also a rectangular box made of corrugated fiberboard, but with plywood trim and a lid open in the half-couch casket style for viewing the body from the waist up. Inside is a fluffy white head roller pad and white dignity comforter, all the container one needs to pay last respects to a loved one, without the indignities of a cardboard box. Wholesale price: $150; expect a

100 percent markup at the mortuary. I asked O'Donnell if she felt elite cardboard box best described the First Step, and she said yes, although fiberboard is a level above cardboard, and added, "I could see my grandmother in that, it wouldn't just be a cardboard box."

Sitting at a table a few feet from the cremation boxes is a young couple at a recording deck. They've been hired to record the memorialites' meetings inside the auditorium, where seventy-five of them are now wrapping up a discussion of their identity crisis, as the conference program puts it, the "explosion of commercial cremation societies," and the "need for Society Standards." The woman is a pretty blond, maybe twenty years old; her boyfriend sits on the table by her side. They seem under the influence of the beautiful summer day, enamored of each other, oblivious to who these people are and why they've brought these casket-like contraptions with them.

The meeting is over, and the memorialites file out of the auditorium. Sprinkled within the crowd of gray and sliver hair are a few women in their thirties and forties, including Karen Leonard, who moves to the First Step table with O'Donnell and her partner and a fortyish woman with short blondish hair and wire rim glasses, whom I'll see later standing directly in front of the cremation box against the wall, measuring it with the top of her head as a frame of reference. I strike up a conversation with Hal Lawson, a retired communications professor who recently joined a memorial society in Flint, Michigan. He tells me: "We're very small, we're trying to grow and find out how some of these organizations have been able to do contracts with funeral homes. Here's a story." Like so many memorialites I meet, Lawson has a negative tale or two about funeral directors. It seems that it's illegal in Michigan to have a contract with funeral homes, as many memorial societies have. "We don't know if it's true that it is illegal in Michigan to contract with a funeral director," Lawson tells me before quickly jumping to a new subject—giant death corporations, a favorite target:

"The three on the stock market, they're taking individual funeral homes and ruining them. We had one very good one in Flint, and they took it over, and just ruined it. . . ."

On a table next to the First Step are memorial society newsletters; copies of Carlson's book and her video, *Tricks of the Funeral Trade*, an overview of the Funeral Rule and the "Funeral Goods and Services" product report from the American Association of Retired Persons. Under "Cautionary notes," the brochure warns: "Some funeral directors may try to shame you, make you feel guilty or simply make it harder for you to choose a lower cost alternative. For these people, the goal is to sell more expensive merchandise with a higher profit margin." Everybody's railing on funeral directors or will be before long, it seems, as Leonard and the Elder Davis team chat by the First Step, and the memorialites spill out into the beautiful day, making their way across the green grass of campus to the dining hall.

TENDING TO YOUR OWN DEAD

I introduce myself to Karen Leonard outside the dining hall, and we sit on a stone wall to chat. She has straight, shoulder-length dirty blond hair, blue eyes, a round face and hunched shoulders. She laughs frequently, a hearty laugh with a momentum of its own, seemingly highly amused and simultaneously outraged at the shenanigans of the funeral director. We pick up where we left off when I was interviewing her on the phone about the tend-to-your-own dead movement in Sonoma County. Leonard doesn't understand why people would think it's unusual or weird to take care of your own dead. It's hard for me to imagine mainstream America suddenly romanticizing about the good old days when grandpa would be laid out in the parlor in a bed of ice while family and friends came for the wake and the undertaker arrived with the casket to take him to the cemetery. In spite of what is said to be the healing effects of washing and dressing the lifeless body of someone you love, maybe even building their coffin and driving them to the cemetery or crematory, I don't imagine most people will be ready to take on this responsibility. But I'm reminded that when cremation started increasing in the 1970s, many people thought it was pagan and unchristian and outrageous and would never become as common as it has. Who's to say the natural death movement has little chance of evolving? Maybe America's ready to face death head on rather than pass it off to the funeral director. England is experiencing a natural death movement, and Carlson is trying to get its Bible, the *Natural Death Handbook*, published here to complement a new edition of her book. Leonard tells me:

> *The memorial societies said you're wasting time and energy on this natural death care, because too few people are going to want this. I always thought that was a false argument. When most of the population doesn't know they can care for their own dead, and those who do know don't know how to do it, how can you honestly say how many people would do it? So, as an experiment in my society, I've been telling them they can care for their own dead and how to go about it. As the years went by, more and more people got involved and decided they wanted to do this. When the consumer understands that they can have a viewing and a full funeral, anything they want, and that they can get out of that trap that we've built in America—this everything-around-embalming thing— then it'll change the whole way we deal with death. We always suspected there would be just a few people who would want to have natural death. The people who would have natural births, the people who want to have control over their lives. Hospice workers. We knew the*

hospice workers would do it because they're not afraid of death. The more death-fearing a culture is, the more likely it's like, 'A dead body in the house, get rid of it!' You know, this reaction we've developed in this culture over time, so that death is so separate from reality, and this fear of death. But we've been amazed by the people who have experienced natural death care, like Jerri [Lyons]. You know, she unzipped the body bag and we were afraid of what we would see, and it wasn't that scary, and it confronted their fear, and it made their ability to deal with death very, very different than just a designed, mass-manufactured ritual that's very expensive, where your rights and choices and actions is a choice of purchasing goods and signing a check.

NATURAL DEATH CARE

It's been two months since I talked to Jerri Lyons about her experience tending to the lifeless body of her holistic hands-on-healing reiki master. I meet her outside the dining hall after an afternoon meeting, and we sit on the bench where I interviewed Carlson. It's late afternoon, the breeze is just the right side of cool and a few stray cumulus clouds float in the sky. Lyons is a slight middle-aged woman with shoulder-length gray hair and dark, moist eyes. She wears purple - knee-length embroidered skirt, tie-died purple blouse, and cardigan sweater. Lyons has been counter-culture since she was a hippie in San Francisco in the 1960s and moved to Oregon and lived in a commune for four years—"We were in the back-to-the-land movement"—where one of her jobs was picking pine cones. By 1976 she and two partners opened a restaurant, The Knight of the Cups, in Coos Bay, and by the mid-1980s she moved back to the Bay area and began studying reiki. Her Rootin' Tootin' Toten Tutors, with Karen Leonard's help, has moved from a ragtag band of wanna-do-gooders, not quite sure how to organize and perform their eclectic mix of clerical, spiritual, and delivery services for the dead, to the official "Natural Death Care Project." Lyons is Project director and one of four natural death care facilitators. A holistic mortician without the merchandise, you might call Lyons. The facilitators had helped tend to nine dead in one way or the other since forming in early 1996, and Lyons was hoping to make this her full-time gig, merging her reiki with this new role as death walker or death midwife, and the meat and potatoes of what the facilitators do—tasks normally performed by the mortician: washing and dressing the body (but never, ever embalming it, that is a four-letter word); loading bodies into their camper and driving them to the crematory; getting death certificates and final disposition permits from town hall and the vital statistics office; and being a calming presence to survivors.

"All we're doing is bringing death back into the family," Lyons tells me. "The traditional funeral of three generations ago is exactly what we're doing. All we're doing in bringing back something that was lost because of money, because of someone preying on people who are vulnerable." Earlier, Carlson had put it to me this way: "In three generations, we've given away the folklore that lets people know what to do at the time of death, and consequently people assume they have to call a funeral director. To some extent, families respond to this helpless mode, perpetrated by the funeral industry—'We'll take care of everything'—when in fact, being physically involved at the time of death takes away the sense of helplessness."

The Project's advisory council includes Leonard, two "thanatologists"—people who study death—someone involved in something called the Life Cycles Educational Program, and a man called Henry Passafero, defined as a "Numismatist, Historian and Financial Planner." At the bottom of the Project's introductory newsletter is a "Traditional Indian Saying": "When you were born/you cried/and the whole world rejoiced/ Live such a life/that when you die/the whole world cries/and you rejoice." The Mission Statement says, "We offer economic, social, and spiritual choices during the sensitive transition time after death and before burial or cremation." The Project hopes to become a nonprofit entity which will let them apply for grants for a vehicle, a gurney—a fancy name for a hospital cot—and other equipment. The facilitators cannot charge for their services because California law says only licensed mortuaries can get paid for providing mortuary services. So they ask clients for a donation, and they've been getting several hundred dollars a case to cover expenses and put a few dollars in their pockets.

Lyons tells me of her experiences with a few clients. One was Tom, in his late thirties, who died of AIDS in the winter of 1996. Lyons had performed reiki on Tom before and after he died. "I was in the room with him and he was dead, and I was sending reiki energy to him, like sending light, to help guide his way, because that time of transition to the next world can be difficult. I felt some kind of presence in the room, I can't really say what it was." When it was time for the crematory, she helped wrap him in a sheet and carry him downstairs with a few other colleagues to his cremation box, which Tom's partner had adorned with a purple towel.

A more recent client of Lyons was twenty-two-year-old Mythris, who died from an overdose of heroin. Her body was brought to the coroner's office for an autopsy. This would be the first time Lyons would see a body in such a state: "I was somewhat nervous about it. It wasn't a pretty sight. I wouldn't want an autopsy for myself or family. They did a blanket stitch to put her back together. It was not pretty." Mythris' mother scrounged up about $450 to cover the cremation and the facilitators' trouble. They took the mother to the coroner's office, helped her fill out paper work to reclaim the body and loaded the body into their camper. The mother wanted to see her daughter, even though she was told that she'd been cut up during the autopsy. In the back of the camper they unzipped the white plastic bag and there was her daughter's body, nude and pale white, "like a China doll," as one of the facilitators put it. The mother let out a few sighs of shock when she saw the top of her daughter's head, which had been stitched back together, sort of sliding around. She recovered, and the facilitators helped her wash the body before they parked the camper at the mother's storage garage, the nearest private spot they could think of, and drew the curtains between the front and back of the camper to give the mother time alone with her daughter. The smells of fragrance and oil filtered into the cab as the mother anointed the body. "We left her alone with her daughter so she could have closure and sing to her, cry with her and do what she needed to do with her," says Lyons. "She had her differences with her daughter, being involved with a crowd who got her involved in drugs. But you love your child no matter what, and to her it meant everything to be able to have that kind of closure, something she never would have gotten if it had been a funeral home that would have just come and got the body from the coroner's office and may or may not have even seen her. But to able to wash it, sing to her and been with her for a while. She wrote a message to her on the top of box, something like, 'Farewell my love, I'll see you on the other side.'" The facilitators' job was over after they drove to the crematory and unloaded Mythris' body.

JOHN BLAKE

John Blake has opened an afternoon session of the memorialite conference with an address he calls, *Cherchez le creaneu*—a hole to fill—in which he'll talk about things like updating databases, reading books on marketing and other tips on running a memorial society. He takes a minute to tell a touching story about the last request of a memorialite who recently died: "He said to her [his wife], 'I want to be cremated, and put my ashes in the trunk of the car, and if you ever get stuck in the winter I'll be there to help you.'" Blake is seventy-five years old, tall and slim, with wire-rim glasses and a mustache, wearing gray slacks and a white sweater. This will be his final talk as executive director after five years at the helm, and when he's finished talking about business matters he tells his audience: "We should be proud that we are volunteers and we are nonprofit, and accept the reality that we are a business. A memorial society shouldn't be a hobby, you must make a commitment."

I remember in my phone conversations with Blake that he was always railing on funeral directors, and only once was I able to get him to concede that there must at least be a few decent ones out there. He wasn't as fanatical as Leonard or Carlson in his diatribes, but he fit the beware-the-mortician mindset of the two dozen or so memorialites I had talked to. Now during his final address, he made it a point to clarify his thoughts on this matter: "Our competition is with high prices. There are many, many fine funeral directors in the country. Compassionate, honest, friendly. They are good guys. I think we make a mistake when we try to place them all in the despicable category." I got a sense Blake's comments were directed to Carlson and Leonard, who are leading FAMSA into the twenty-first century on a platform of attacking the money-making schemes of the death industry. As much as memorialites villainize funeral directors, many of them simply want to get their members to plan for the inevitable and to not get taken. They have no interest in lobbying their state senator to put pressure on the funeral board to lift the rule that forbids cemeteries from selling caskets. Who has time to tip off scandal-monger reporters about the funeral home that charged $1,500 for a cremation? As Carolyn Burke, executive secretary of the

Memorial and Planned Funeral Society of St. Louis, told me about her members: "They want a good deal so they plan ahead." It's all about getting people information, the nonconfrontational memorialites tell me, and this doesn't necessarily preclude information about what a swindler Joe Blow funeral director is.

Mercedes Bern-King, a young social worker on the board of the memorial society in Kansas City, Missouri, stood when Blake opened up the floor to comments and said: "Low income people truly need this information. And in Kansas City, it's the chaplains and priests who have been hungry for the kind of information we have. They have no idea that consumers have so much choice. So, yes, continue doing the good cremation work, but also I think we need to appeal to whatever kind of final arrangement people want, and help them get what they want by letting them know." Jim, a Unitarian and memorial society treasurer, told me, "our constituency is people who are generally fairly old, do not attend meetings, pay their dues, and they just want the best deal that's possible."

Some memorialites are wary of Carlson's call to arms, like Roland "Knob" Knobles of the Memorial Society of Atlanta, one of the country's largest with 5,300 members. Knob, and he insists you call him this, is a semiretired professor of health administration at Emery University. I met him early one morning in the parlor of the administration building where he was sitting with a few people in front of a fireplace. We talked a bit about his church, he's a Unitarian, and then I asked him if he's as wary as Carlson is about the Everyman mortician. No, as a matter of fact, Knob said, he works with six funeral homes in the greater Atlanta area, all compassionate fellows with reasonable prices. One charges just $100 for cremation in AIDS cases. It's the type of thing Carlson and Leonard no doubt don't want to hear. Their crusade seems to be to malign the industry by constantly painting it as rotten to the core.

I called Carlson after the conference to get her response to the fact that not all her people are on board her bandwagon, and she immediately started in with a sneaky funeral director trick I hadn't yet heard: "A lot of the people who think everything is fine are not informed of the FTC loopholes, like letting funeral directors not include the price of the actual cremation for an immediate cremation." She explained that some mortuaries charge one fee for a direct cremation, say $1,000, which is on the high end, and then charge another $300 or so as a cash advance fee for the cremation itself. "They can call it a cash advance item, give me a fucking break," Carlson railed, and went on, "Some of the people who think every thing is hunky dory haven't spent as much time as Karen and I studying the mischief."

Carlson finally said something good about funeral directors after I brought up for a second and third time that some memorialites have very good relationships with them: "A disaster like the Oklahoma City bombing brings out the best in all of them," referring to how they volunteered their services identifying the dead and counseling survivors in the aftermath of the bombing.

RIP-OFF, RIP-OFF, RIP-OFF

I am introduced to the world of sixty-six-year-old Fr. Henry Wasielewski by Karen Leonard, who has put his World Wide Web site, "Funeral and Ripoffs," on the screen in the conference center auditorium during a nighttime program. Fr. Henry has become a bit of a legend for the mortician-hating crowd, and now Leonard is introducing him to the memorialites. The site is a collection of thirty pages (at last count) with scathing indictments against the funeral industry. "This is the first time casket wholesale prices have ever been revealed in the U.S.," declares a page Leonard has called up with the heading,

"Extortionist markups, profits." "These 1995 wholesale prices are correct within a few percentage points throughout the country. For the first time in U.S. history, this document and price chart provided to the nation's media, the casket wholesale prices and markups which the funeral industry has for decades kept top-secret . . . keeping wholesale prices absolutely secret from the media is the only way mortuaries can continue unhindered to rip off nearly every U.S. citizen with extortionist, 300 to 900 percent markups. The entire industry, casket manufacturers and 22,000 mortuaries . . . have worked together throughout this century to keep these prices a secret from the media and prevent the public from learning of the injustice . . ." Leonard tells the audience: "When I was doing undercover in San Francisco," recalling her early days as proprietor of an avant garde retail casket store, when she spied on funeral homes to get their prices, "we were seeing, at an average, five to six time markups on caskets." So much has been written since the early 1960s about huge casket markups, and so many lines of cheap caskets and cremation boxes have been introduced since, that it's remarkable that death industry foes keep hammering away at the "extortionist" price of caskets.

Fr. Henry's condemnations are relentless. He's retired now with plenty of time to tinker on the internet and indulge his passion of trashing the funeral industry, which he's been doing publicly since the early 1980s when he started something he calls the Interfaith Funeral Information Committee. "He has suffered a great deal of exorcism by the Church itself," explains Leonard as she maneuvers the computer mouse around Fr. Henry's pages. "They keep putting him in smaller and smaller parishes, farther and father in the desert. And I said, 'I'm sorry Henry about what's happening to you,' and he says, 'But they don't understand: Now I have more time to investigate the industry.'" This draws thunderous laughter from the crowd. "And so now he's in a trailer somewhere in Arizona, and give him a computer and he is one happy man. He's a wonderful guy, and he will talk your ear off."

It seemed like not thirty seconds went by during a phone conversation I had with Fr. Henry after the conference without him saying the word *ripoff*. And, by the way, he told me, he hasn't lived in the trailer Leonard mentioned for about eight years, and, in case I cared, it served as his rectory in the little town of Guadalupe, Arizona. "I got started because of the ripoffs of people in the parish," Fr. Henry explained. "We had a parish with a lot of funerals. One day they'd say the price was $1,000; the next day the same funeral was $2,000, and the next it was $3,000. And I thought this was crazy, these were poor people. This is cruel, and this is what I keep finding. I decided people shouldn't get ripped off. The ripoffs don't stop. They get worse and worse. No matter where you turn. Ripoff ads in the newspapers. The National Funeral Directors Association is a ripoff artist—the kind of booklets they put out. . . ."

Even Fr. Henry's fellow Roman Catholic priests should be ashamed of themselves, he says, for collusion with the bad guys: "The Church is very involved in funerals. The Church is very involved with the funeral industry. Ripping off people is taking place right inside the church; priests and ministers are taking bribes from the morticians and helping morticians with the ripoff." Responding to Fr. Henry's hit, Fr. Michael Diskin, assistant chancellor for the Roman Catholic Diocese of Phoenix, told me: "We're not aware of anything to substantiate his allegations. He has a right to his opinions."

His ripoff comments just kept coming:

"They rip off some poor family every two weeks, that is a crime. . . ."

"Rich people can get ripped off and it doesn't bother them. But we have parishes with loads of poor people, and they are getting ripped off . . .

Yes, says Fr. Henry, virtually all morticians are ripoffs, consciously bamboozling an unsuspecting public: "Maybe five percent are not ripoffs," he calculates.

Hating funeral directors may have begun for Fr. Henry thirty years ago when he was shopping with his father for a funeral for his mother. "They tried to sell us protective caskets back then," he remembers. "They got us started with the highest priced one, and then they said this is the last one with a neoprene seal. My dad was about to fall apart. It was torture for my dad. He was being taken down this road with the high-priced caskets and this one, and I could just see my dad feeling badly that some how he couldn't afford these, and he'd have to take a cheaper one. I thought: 'We don't need to know about neoprene seals, why bring it up?' "

THE BBC TRASHES AMERICA'S DEATH INDUSTRY

It was time for a few laughs, and entertainment would be provided by the recent BBC documentary, *Over My Dead Body*, courtesy of Lisa Carlson and Karen Leonard. About fifty memorialites gather around a small television in a room above the auditorium as Carlson introduces the piece and the show begins. The piece has cameo appearances by Jessica Mitford, a native of England and now a dignified little old lady who took her cause celebre with her into her final years. One scene has her making fun of a British undertaker as he shows her caskets, and she appears again at the end having tea with a friend in a cemetery discussing the merits of socializing the business of death. Part of the piece focuses on the Americanization of the British funeral industry: In 1994, Service Corporation International of Houston acquired 534 of Great Britain's funeral homes (and a smattering of cemeteries and crematoria). "The Americans have arrived," reads a caption over an American flag draped on a casket, and the Memorialites respond with hearty laughter. "This casket is $59,500," says a funeral director at the upper crust Frank E. Campbell Funeral Home on the Upper East Side of Manhattan, one of SCI's prized operations, showing the BBC interviewer around the place. This brings another chorus of laughs. "This one is made of cast bronze, this is slightly under a ton in weight. It's the top of the line for us at $85,000."

The documentary takes us to the New Jersey funeral director's death show in Atlantic City, with the casketeers, vault people, and death dresses encountered in Chapter One. The narrator, with his serious voice and crisp accent befitting Monty Python, points out: "And it's not just caskets. [There are] suits and gowns especially designed for corpses." The memorialites break out in hysterics as a man at a booth demonstrates hand cream for the dead. More loud laughter comes when we hear a woman introduce a television report from a cemetery: "Now the Mount Olivet report. 'Hi, this is Denise reporting from Mount Olivet, where many exciting things are happening.'" We're taken to the Dallas Institute of Funeral Service in Texas and told, "Student undertakers learn everything from removing a face to the more important funeral sales psychology." The documentary takes a hit at America's "Aftercare" cottage industry that's sprung up in the last ten or fifteen years: "Undertakers here don't just dispose of the dead these days, they also look after those who have been left behind . . . Undertakers use it not only as advertising for their business, but also use it to try to sell their preneed funeral payment schemes to grieving relatives. Paying in advance for your funeral they say can be therapeutic."

The BBC says Americans spend $14 billion a year on death—it's actually closer to $12 billion—and concludes: "But one choice that does not seem to be available to the American consumer is buying a cheap funeral: The average cost is about $6,000. And American undertakers have been known to react badly when people don't pay up." More laughter from the audience as footage of an American TV news reporter appears: "The man died Friday of cancer and was taken to Evans Mortuary where he was supposed to be cremated. But his body was dumped on the doorstep of his home when his son couldn't afford to pay all of the costs."

SHADY CHARACTER

It began for Philip Towle of Rindge, New Hampshire, more than sixty years ago, when he was a student at Albion College in Michigan studying electrical engineering. I met Rindge, a feisty eighty-year-old Quaker wearing a blue pin-stripe blazer and white turtleneck, in the auditorium after Carlson's call to arms. Every time I saw Towle he was smiling and laughing, the kind of thick mirthful laugh that's contagious. He began to tell me the story of how he got involved with memorial societies in 1970 when he needed to have his eleven-year-old son's body moved from the medical hospital where it was being used for research to a cemetery, and a funeral director wanted to charge him $700 to transport it. He went ahead and tried to take the body even after Towle told him not to. He eventually hired a black funeral director to move the body for $250. When I called Towle after the convention I found out that his story actually began in the late 1930s in Albion, Michigan, where he worked a few hours each week at a funeral home while earning his degree. There was "a second funeral director in town," Towle said, "very crooked, he would be there at a fatal accident, and sneak away bodies, and he'd tell the cops, I'll take care of it. Oh, he was a shady character."

His career moved from engineering to teaching, and he taught elementary school students in Kenya for seven years in the 1960s. Since 1970 he's been teaching handicapped students at the Crotched Mountain Rehabilitation Center, where he still works every day. He's wound down his activity with various New England memorial societies, and knows it's time to make final plans.

"Let's face it," he told me, "Here I am eighty years old, and I'm swimming three-quarters of a mile almost every day. But the time'll come . . . if I can get in with one of medical universities, I want them to work on me."

EPILOGUE

The U.S. death industry plods along quietly setting about the task of providing the ways and means of tending to our dead. Expect ongoing scandal, like the New Jersey cemetery burying people under sidewalks, the swindler in Southern California taking the cemetery endowment funds and running, the crematory cremating bodies en masse, the mortician bilking the unsuspecting bereaved into pricey funerals. Scandal is a given in any industry, and despite what's being sold, the death industry is just that, and the people in it carry similar drives, ambitions, and temptations as anyone in a profit-driven enterprise.

It's unlikely mainstream America will start tending to its own dead, despite the efforts of the left-wing memorialites. Lisa Carlson made a splash on national television nearly ten years ago with her book, *Caring for Your Own Dead*. Today there's still only a handful of communities like Sonoma County, California, where the group that began as the Rootin' Tootin' Totum Tutors are at work.

Expect plenty of eccentric death rituals, along the lines of a pinch of Timothy Leary's mortal remains blasted into orbit and someone choosing to be buried in a favorite car. And it's just a matter of time before Corky Ra and John Chew produce their first mummy.

Each year it will be more likely that the funeral director you call will work for one of the giant death corporations, as five of them have been on aggressive acquisition rolls for the past ten years and as of mid-1996 owned about 18 percent of America's 23,000 funeral homes. Also expect the American way of death to continue being exported around the world. Service Corporation International of Houston owns 534 funeral homes in the United Kingdom and 1,000 in France and one hundred or so in Australia. In June 1996, Stewart Enterprises of New Orleans, had acquired five funeral homes in New Zealand to add to its roster of 200 mortuaries and 120 cemeteries in the U.S., Mexico, Puerto Rico, and Australia.

If you're a traditionalist and want your body in the ground, or want to bury rather than cremate loved ones, there's plenty of cemetery land in most areas of the country, despite warnings that we're running out of space for the dead, although it'll be expensive in urban areas. The same goes for above-ground interments, with mausolea and lawn crypts popping up at cemeteries throughout the land.

There's never been more variety in death merchandise. A return to chapters one and two should convince you of this. The free market is working in a frenzy in the area of con-tainerization for dead bodies; Americans have as much choice in caskets and cremation boxes as they do for any of our must-have purchases. The same goes for vaults and grave liners, which you almost always must have if your body or cremains are going in the ground. Urns are selling like hot cakes, and everyone from ceramics artists to giant casketeers are making them.

Billions of dollars are being spent on pay-before-you-die funeral plans, and the local cemetery is likely to have memori-al counselors (or boiler room telemarketers) dialing your num-ber to pitch you your grave before it's too late and one of your grieving survivors is left with this most unwanted task. If you're bereaved and hurting, and the comforting hand of the town mortician isn't enough, or if you don't happen to know any comforting morticians and you're not so devastated that you need therapy, America now has a cottage industry of companies offering aftercare services.

And year after year the death shows will travel to America's great cities in a celebration of the merchandising of death that could only happen here.

SOURCES

Many of the sources used in this book are mentioned as they are used in the text. Following is a list of material I drew on for historical sections, including some sources mentioned in the text:

Habenstein, Robert W., and William M. Lamers. *Funeral Customs The World Over*. Milwaukee: Bulfin Printers Inc., 1994.

Habenstein, Robert W., and William M. Lamers. *The History of American Funeral Directing*. Milwaukee: National Funeral Directors Association, 1995.

Irion, Paul E. *Cremation*. Philadelphia: Fortress Press, 1968.

Iserson, Kenneth V. *Death to Dust: What Happens to Dead Bodies*. Tucson: Galen Press, 1994.

Le Moyne, F. Julius. *An Argument to Prove That Cremation is Preferable to Inhumation of Dead Bodies*. Pittsburgh: E. W. Lightner, editor and publisher, 1878.

Mayer, Robert G. *Embalming History, Theory, and Practice*. East Norwalk, Conn.: Appleton & Lange, 1990.

Noll, the Rev. Arthur Howard. *The Western Undertaker*, Vol. 23, Oct. 1903, P. 7.; and various *Western Undertaker* volumes from 1903 and 1909.

Puckle, Bertram. *Funeral Customs: Their Origin & Development*. London: T. Werner Laurie, 1926.

Sloane, David Charles. *The Last Great Necessity: Cemeteries in American History*. Baltimore: John Hopkins University Press, 1995.

Svanevik, Michael and Shirley Burgett. *City of Souls: San Francisco's Necropolis at Colma*. San Francisco: Custom and Limited Editions, 1995.

Other trade publications and newsletters referenced:

American Blue Book of Funeral Directors
American Cemetery
American Funeral Director
Catholic Cemetery, publication of the National Catholic
    Cemetery Conference
The Embalmers' Monthly, May 1914
Funeral Insider newsletter
Funeral Monitor newsletter
Pharos International, journal of the Cremation Association of
    Great Britain and the International Cremation Federation
Background material was used from publications of the
    following:
American Cemetery Association, Reston, Va.
Casket and Funeral Supply Association of America
Cremation Association of North America, Chicago
Federal Trade Commission, Funeral Rule Violation Press
    Releases, Washington, D.C.
Federated Funeral Directors of America, Springfield, Ill.
Hillenbrand Industries 1995 Annual Report, Batesville, Ind.
Lynn University, Funeral Service Department, Boca Raton,
    Fla.
National Foundation of Funeral Service, Des Plaines, Ill.
National Funeral Directors Association, Milwaukee, Wis.
Service Corp. International 1995 Annual Report, Houston.
Summum Corporation, Salt Lake City, Utah